Overcoming the Blues

Finding Christ-Centered Hope and Joy through Serving Others

Ryan Noel Fraser, PhD

Foreword by Cecil Murphey

Good Books

New York, New York

Good Books books may be purchased in bulk at special
discounts for sales promotion, corporate gifts, fund-raising, or
educational purposes. Special editions can also be created to
specifications. For details, contact the Special Sales Department,
Good Books, 307 West 36th Street, 11th Floor, New York, NY
10018 or info@skyhorsepublishing.com.

Good Books is an imprint of Skyhorse Publishing, Inc.®, a
Delaware corporation.

Visit our website at www.goodbooks.com.

10 9 8 7 6 5 4 3 2 1

Library of Congress Cataloging-in-Publication Data is available
on file.

Cover design by Peter Donahue
Cover photo by gettyimages

Print ISBN: 978-1-68099-486-5
Ebook ISBN: 978-1-68099-487-2

Printed in the United States of America

To Missy, my Kansas sunflower

Contents

The ideas presented in this book are in no way intended to be a replacement for proper medical care (including medication) or for specialized, professional counseling/psychotherapy. If you feel like you are in imminent danger of harming yourself or someone else, please seek professional help immediately. You are valuable and your life is too precious to put at risk. The National Suicide Prevention Lifeline is 1-800-273-8255 (available 24/7, toll-free). Their website is: www.SuicidePreventionLifeline.org.

Foreword

"WHAT'S wrong with me?"

This is a common question from people who suffer from depression. I heard that many times from my late wife, Shirley, who suffered with bouts of the Blues. Shirley and others tend to start with self-blame. "If I were all that I should be . . ." Once they make such statements, they find endless ways to focus on their own shortcomings.

I reminded Shirley that we can't change our basic nature. Some people are prone to depression just as some have varicose veins or poor eyesight. We all have emotional or physical weaknesses that aren't our fault. My good friend Stan Cottrell is a professional runner, yet he struggles with controlling his cholesterol—a proclivity he inherited from his dad.

If you're prone to depression, rather than focus on what's wrong with you, Dr. Ryan Fraser offers valuable suggestions on how to change your perspective. One way to start is to say, "I am depressed. It's a normal, human emotion." If you can accept that it's not something you caused, you can begin to avoid the poor-me syndrome.

My wife learned to say (often many times a day), "My feelings are my emotions; they are not reality." By that, she referred to her sense of uselessness, sadness, and feelings of no self-worth. Or as she said, "The more I can do for myself, the more I can shake those haunting inner voices. I try to focus on giving and not on receiving."

As Dr. Fraser advocates in *Overcoming the Blues*, she focused on others as much as possible. Simple things like sending get-well cards or calling people she hadn't seen at church. She participated in church activities, such as women's Bible study.

As her health deteriorated, every morning—regardless of her negative emotions—she went into her office, pulled out the church directory, and prayed down the list for each member by name. She said it usually took her three days to cover everyone. Then she started again.

I strongly agree with what Dr. Fraser says you can do for yourself.

Exercise. It's not easy to get started on a daily exercise program. Enlist a friend to help.

Learn to eat healthy. Avoid resorting to the so-called comfort foods. Emphasize nutritional meals.

Get enough sleep. That posed the most trouble for Shirley. By not napping during the day, she was tired at night and slept better.

In *Overcoming the Blues*, Fraser offers a number of practical tasks you can do for yourself and others. Consider them carefully. You may not be able to cure yourself, but you can certainly manage your depression.

—Cecil Murphey
USA Today and *New York Times* bestselling author and
coauthor of 140 books, including *Gifted Hands: The Ben Carson Story; 90 Minutes in Heaven,* and *People I Met at the Gates of Heaven: Who Will Be There Because of You?*

Introduction

YOU are depressed. You're feeling down and disillusioned—even despondent. You're extremely discouraged. Your energy level is at an all-time low. Your body is literally aching inside and out. And your heart is hurting. Life is hard for you. Really, really hard. And you're struggling to make sense of it all. More than that, your faith is perhaps floundering, even gradually disintegrating bit by bit. You feel lost, confused, angry, and alone. You crave some kind of immediate relief, respite for your soul, but don't know exactly what to do about your seemingly hopeless situation or where to turn for help.

Don't worry! Help is on its way! But it is aid of a different kind. It is relief that comes from a unique and unexpected place—a fresh perspective on your depression and psychological and spiritual recovery process. This book is about transformation. It's about personal growth. It's about rising above your own emotional pain and meeting a spiritual challenge head-on.

I want to help you deepen your faith, increase your compassion, and strengthen your care. Not *in spite of* depression, but precisely *because of* it. Now, I certainly don't intend in any way to trivialize depression or downplay its seriousness (see Appendix on page 161 for stats), nor am I advocating that people abandon their medical doctors' orders, including necessary prescriptions. This is a book about how to live faithfully as a believer while struggling with depression at whatever level—whether mild, moderate, or severe.

Those who suffer with depression possess an emotional connection and sense of solidarity with fellow sufferers. If you're reading this book, it's likely that you either struggle with depression or are concerned about someone close to you who does. I know it's a great concern to you. Hope is often eroded, sometimes all but destroyed, by depression. As you may know from your own painful experience, an individual's personal sense of well-being and self-esteem are frequently dismantled when depression gets the upper hand. Like a solar eclipse, the light of day is vanquished by impenetrable darkness. A shadow suddenly sweeps over the sufferer, infiltrating every single nook and cranny of his or her existence. For some, this experience can be absolutely terrifying, but your battle with the blues presents you with a unique opportunity to grow as an individual. To love more sincerely. To reach out with the compassion of Christ. To possess his heart and be his hands in this world in a more potent and meaningful way than ever before in your life. Depression can be a doorway to greater depth and discovery. The apostle Paul states something rather revolutionary:

> Blessed be the God and Father of our Lord Jesus Christ, the Father of mercies and God of all comfort, who comforts us in all our affliction, so that we may be able to comfort those who are in any affliction, with the comfort with which we ourselves are comforted by God. For as we share abundantly in Christ's sufferings, so through Christ we share abundantly in comfort too. (2 Cor. 1:3-5 English Standard Version)

In Paul's way of thinking that suffering produces an increased sensitivity to the needs of others, deeper compassion, and a greater capacity for spiritual care and comfort, one of the most effective strategies for coping with the blues in your own life is to shift your perspective by taking your eyes off self and turning your heart's attention toward others and their needs. Serving can be more than merely a short-lived distraction from your own suffering; it can act as a powerful and restorative antidote. It can be a transformative way of life that facilitates healing, health, and hope.

So, are you ready for something different? Are you wanting a positive and proactive change in your life? If so, prepare for an unparalleled and extremely challenging but extraordinarily fulfilling journey. Get ready to flex your faith, build your spiritual muscles, and move out of the dark shadows of your (dis)comfort zone. It's time for you to grow!

There are numerous ways others have suggested to combat depression, such as basking in the sunlight, listening to uplifting music, taking up a hobby, getting involved in the arts, exercising regularly, or reading a good book. Additional strategies include such things as immersing yourself in nature, taking a candlelit bath, learning a new language, escaping through entertainment, journaling, talking positively to yourself, getting a massage, aromatherapy, praise and worship, memorizing Scripture, developing mantras, and looking for glimpses of God. These ideas all have merit, but I'd like to challenge you in three distinct ways:

1. to *recognize* God's abiding presence,
2. to *reconnect by reaching out* to others, and
3. to *respect* your own limitations.

§

The God of All Comfort

It's important, first of all, to *recognize* that despite the emotional pain and distress produced by depression, God's abiding presence remains and he is going to take care of you no matter what happens. Spiritual peace is fostered through a trusting relationship with God.

The Bible demonstrates that God desires a deeper and more intimate relationship with you as his beloved child.

Although depression often sabotages your ability to respond to God's loving overtures, he is in relentless pursuit of you. The source of your strength is God's unfailing love in your life. My intention in employing scriptures in this book is solely for the purpose of providing much-needed encouragement and hope. I am drawing on the Word of God to demonstrate his deep empathy and unlimited compassion for his children who suffer with depression. When you hurt, he hurts. When you cry, he cries. The scriptures are not being employed to point fingers, cast blame, minimize your problem, or guilt you into feeling worse for experiencing the pain of depression in your life. God's inspired Word is included here to supply new life and spiritual sustenance.

David was a man after God's heart, but one who struggled at times with depression. He models for us an authentic and honest relationship with the Lord. Rather than attempting to hide his melancholy heart, he was open about his darkest emotions. The psalms he penned are beautifully transparent and so sincere and poignant that it seems he lends words to our own thoughts and feelings. David's primary strategy against depression was prayer and worship. Elijah's story in the Old Testament confirms this deep truth. Prayer is a powerful tool for combating loneliness since God is always listening.

Second, it is critical to *reconnect* to your loved ones and foster deeper levels of intimacy with your friends. *Reach out* to them and to others who may be discouraged. Though we will offer more examples further on in the book, a simple example would be to drop a card in the mail. Though we live in a day and age where technology seems to rule supreme and most personal communications are handled electronically (via emails, texts, or messaging), people still appreciate receiving a handwritten note or card of encouragement in their mailbox. It's something tangible they treasure, a kind expression of Christian love, which can make a positive difference for them. By your going to the trouble, it shows that you care enough to go the extra mile in demonstrating your genuine concern and/or appreciation for them. They will feel affirmed and valued.

Third, it is essential that you *respect* your own limitations. Since there are definite limits to your physical and emotional energy resources, it is important to maintain healthy personal and interpersonal boundaries. This requires appropriate self-love and self-care. It's nearly impossible to be there for others, when you're not first there for yourself. Proper preventative medical care (including regular check-ups and taking prescribed medication) and professional counseling are also vehicles through which God's sustaining grace is provided. Knowing your boundaries and respecting your limitations demonstrates maturity, self-awareness, and wisdom. Jesus once said to "Love your neighbor as yourself" (Mark 12:31). This commandment implies self-love at its core, so as to allow for the possibility of loving and caring for others.

God loves you and hasn't abandoned you despite your depression. He has put this book in your hands to help you find a hope-filled path toward emotional and spiritual healing. The Creator of heaven and earth is lovingly initiating into your life today. Now it's up to you how you will choose to respond. God is doing His part. Will you do yours?

§

A Note about Blue Tasks

At the end of each chapter, I include a "blue task" as an ongoing part of your journey toward overcoming the blues. It is my hope that you will complete this task before moving on to the next chapter. I encourage you to pick one task to start with. If you're only able to do one, that is perfectly okay. Complete more tasks as you feel you are able. After you finish reading this book, the blue tasks will remain integral to your recovery process. Return to the blue tasks on a regular basis and continue to work on them consistently. The blue tasks should not be considered works of completion, but works in progress.

Chapter One

The Beginning

I'M trying to remember back to the first time it happened. She had been mad before, but not *this* mad. She had been sad before, but not *this* sad. One day she confessed, when the children were little, she would buckle them into their booster seats, but leave her own seatbelt unclicked on purpose. Though she wasn't actively suicidal, in her despair, she'd hoped God would take her so she could escape the intense emotional pain. We cried together that day, and she promised me she wouldn't do that again. The children needed her, and I did too.

My precious Missy was slipping into the dark indigo (one of the shades of blue explained in chapter seven) and I didn't know how to help, which is hard for me to say. My job is helping people. I help people fix their marriages. I help them with their rebellious teenagers. I help them cope with anxiety and panic attacks. I help businessmen learn to self-calm. I help law enforcement officers manage their anger. I help the grieving widow and widower. I even help others with depression. But this was different. This was the love of my life, my soulmate, and my best friend. Somehow, I couldn't help her. I was at a complete loss on how to intervene.

We had had a very difficult year. And when I say *difficult*, it doesn't seem to do that year justice. We learned to rate her days. To evaluate them based on how deep into the blue she was.

This is what we would call a *dark indigo* year, the deepest shade before everything goes black.

It all started June 20th, 2005. Our son, Austin, at the age of four, was having severe health problems, Missy's precious mother, Jeannie, passed away unexpectedly, and my Missy's kidneys were failing. It was all too much! She had sunk into the dark indigo and I wasn't sure how to bring her back. How could I reach her?

§

It resembled the story of the Jewish prophet Jeremiah who was thrown into a waterless cistern and sank into the mire (Jeremiah 38). There was no way for him to get out. He needed help. Jeremiah was extremely weak, hadn't eaten anything in days, and couldn't feel his legs. He was stuck and he knew it. How long would it take him to die in the solitary confinement of the dark cistern, cold and alone in the mud, abandoned? The strength would not come from within. He had none left. Jeremiah would require help—help from above, so God sent Ebed-melech the Ethiopian, a eunuch who was in King Zedekiah's house, to tell Jeremiah what to do. Ebed-melech then came with thirty men. Jeremiah wondered if he was hallucinating, but when Ebed-melech lowered down the makeshift fabric rope, he felt it. That cloth cord was his only hope of getting out of this deathtrap. But could he make himself do what he needed to in order to help himself survive?

Ebed-melech was shouting, "Put it around your waist and under your arms!"

It all sounded so simple, so why couldn't he get his body to respond and do what his mind wanted so desperately to do?

You know, we've all heard it before: "Just be grateful for the help. Take it and get better. Just put on your big boy/girl pants and get over it." But how? When had everything become so difficult?

2

Jeremiah was once a strong and vibrant prophet, and now the weight of the fabric seemed to crush him, but slowly he worked it around his waist and looped it under his arms. Then, Ebed-melech and his helpers began the slow and painful process of hoisting Jeremiah up and out of the pit. As he moved upward, he caught a glimpse of the cobalt sky and began to feel a small seed of hope growing within him.

§

Have you been there? Or have you seen someone you love sinking deep into the dark indigo and felt helpless? I have. I pray that you find seeds of hope to help your spouse, your coworker, friend, parent, child, or even yourself. Like grief, depression moves through stages. You will become familiar with the different shades of blue as you read this book.

Let's begin with perhaps the most difficult part of your journey: caring for yourself. You see, often the one battling with depression is a good caregiver. They care for others well. But they struggle with being on the receiving end of care. They find it hard to ask for help.

Depression, like any illness, can affect anyone. The CEO who can take care of his business in his sleep, the mother who takes meticulous care of all her children's and husband's needs, the straight-A student who serves on the student government, the nurse who provides excellent care to her sick patients, or the minister who looks after the spiritual needs of his congregation.

I'm here to tell you something important. God has placed me here for this purpose and this time. You are a child of God. You are a son or daughter of the King of kings. You are a promised gift to this world. Therefore, you are worthy of care. But, before you can care for anyone or anything else—your business, your career, your family, your students, your patients, your customers, your employees, your church, or even your pet—you must first realize how important you are to God. You see, you are His! You were created for a special purpose, just like Esther was brought to the throne for "such a time as this" (Esther 4:14).

§

Imagine for a minute that a king sent out a proclamation to all the land. He was looking for someone to take care of his little daughter. He wanted this person to be kind to her, to forgive her of her faults, to nurture her growth in mind, body, and spirit, to make sure she had superb medical care, and give her the best nourishment possible. Applicants responded throughout the kingdom. Though many responded, only one was selected. It was you. You were the one chosen to care for the child of the king. And, my precious friend, you are that child.

Like Ebed-melech did for Jeremiah, I'm lowering you a lifeline, a way up. Please find the strength to secure it. Let me help you out of the pit you're in.

§

It Starts with Self-Care
Many people feel like they're being selfish if they invest any time, energy, or resources into taking care of their own emotional and spiritual needs, but to care for yourself is to care for God's precious child. It is to treasure his beloved offspring and spiritual heir.

Self-care takes many forms: physical, emotional, intellectual, relational, and spiritual. It involves caring for your body, your heart, your mind, and your soul and spirit. Think back to a time when you felt better. What is it you were doing at that time that made you feel good? Ask yourself the following questions:

- Were you participating with others in a benevolence project?

4

- Were you enjoying a particular activity such as your favorite sport or hobby?
- Were you eating healthier and exercising more regularly?
- Were you pampering yourself on a consistent basis? For example, going to the gym, beauty parlor, or spa?
- Were you taking time to smell the roses, or going to the river or lake to fish, to watch the ducks swimming, or just to sit and watch children playing?
- Were you going golfing with your buddies once a week?
- Were you going on occasional shopping trips to the outlet mall with the girls?
- Were you working on creative projects out in the garage or workshop?
- Were you painting, sculpting, or making pottery?
- Were you going out to concerts or sporting events, or out to eat with friends?
- Were you watching a particular sitcom or reading a certain genre of non-work-related books?

If you've answered "Yes" to any of the above questions, compare your life from back then to the present day. When did you begin backing off these activities and engaging in them less often? Did something happen to throw you off your game or derail you? And why did you ultimately quit? Did it happen gradually or all of a sudden? What was it that interfered and got in the way of your happiness?

Now, make a written list of every item you can think of that applies (and any other clue you can possibly think of) on a piece of paper or your electronic device. The list needs to have two columns: the first should be labeled, "Things I used to do for myself that I enjoyed"; and the second can be labeled, "Things that sabotaged my happiness." Once you have the list written, put a checkmark beside or highlight the items in the first column that you would like to re-implement in your life. Next, carefully choose three of the items you are prepared to commit to and will actively pursue in the coming week to practice better self-care. Sound like a workable plan? At the end of the first week of making some much-needed changes, you may add a few items to the list, but not so many as to feel overwhelmed. This isn't supposed to feel like a chore or burden, but a proactive strategy, because before you can really reach out to others with Christ's love and compassion, you must first learn to extend that same type of love and compassion to yourself. Again, remember that you are a beloved child of God and belong to him. Therefore, you're worth it and deserve it.

§

Blue Task
#1

- Go to my YouTube channel (Ryan Noel Fraser, PhD) and listen to the song for Blue Task #1. Think about the words and how they apply to your own life.
- You may choose to add the song to your personal playlist and listen to it as needed throughout the day. Music can touch the soul in a powerful way and minister to your spirit.
- Next, share that (or another) song with someone else that may stand to benefit emotionally and spiritually from hearing it and being edified through it.
- On my website, RyanNoelFraser.com, post the title of a song that has encouraged you to keep going. Alternately, make a phone call to check on someone that you're concerned about and tell him or her that you care. You can even offer to pray for the person over the telephone, if appropriate.

Chapter Two

The Positives of Depression

LIVING with depression isn't easy. In this chapter, I will ask you to try and see the good in your struggle. I know this may sound crazy. And let me be abundantly clear that I would never want anyone to suffer with depression, but since you do, or someone you love does, I'm going to ask you to lay aside your preconceived notions about this debilitating disease for a moment. And I'm going to challenge you to think outside the box by looking beyond the conventional ways of dealing with it.

Our first step together will be searching for the good among the bad. It may be difficult to see anything good ever coming from depression. To even entertain the thought of such a thing being a remote possibility seems counterintuitive. When one thinks about dealing with the blues, the tendency is to focus only on the noticeable negatives. But for every negative, there is generally also a positive. Now, please understand that I intend in no way to downplay or trivialize the intense emotional pain and serious difficulties associated with the symptoms of depression, nor do I wish to insult your intelligence. My purpose, however, is to challenge your thinking and reframe your perspective just enough to make room for some new possibilities. I want you to look at depression from a fresh perspective. Because—sure enough—if we gaze hard enough together, we will be able to discover some helpful aspects to struggling with the blues. I view each of these hidden facets as a potential opportunity for personal development. As the old saying goes, "Every dark cloud has a silver lining." Please hear me out before you make up your mind. This will likely be different from anything you've ever heard before.

§

Over the years, I've worked in faith-based clinical mental health settings and, more recently, in private practice with hundreds of believers who suffer with depression. At times I've struggled with how to respond appropriately. My faith has definitely been challenged in the process. Trying to grasp the immensity of their struggles and uncover potential paths to their recovery has been challenging. However, my clients' amazing courage in the midst of unimaginable emotional duress has been inspiring to me. I have learned a lot from my clients' remarkable stories and their faithful resilience under trying circumstances. For this blessing I'm truly thankful.

I'd like to provide a dose of much-needed encouragement. Depression offers us the chance to grow in our understanding of God, self, and others. Introspection is a catalyst for digging deeper spiritually, emotionally, and relationally. Yes, the painful experience of depression carries within it the inherent power to heighten your awareness of not only your own suffering, but also of the struggles of those around you. It intensifies your ability to authentically sympathize and empathize with other individuals who are also going through difficult times in their lives. It gives you "insider" knowledge. This experiential knowledge or rather practical wisdom is a powerful resource holding within it a great potential for good!

Remember, the presence of depression in your life isn't indicative of God's judgment or disapproval. As your loving and compassionate father, God cares deeply about you and hurts for you in the midst of your struggle. He cares more deeply than your depression can go. Yet, depression doesn't need to define your life. It's just one facet of the overall picture and not the sum of who you are. It is only a part of your identity and not all of you. It doesn't need to define your walk with God, either. In fact, it can push you to a deeper walk.

§

More Than Conquerors in Christ

It's not uncommon for suffering Christians to have the following kinds of unhealthy ruminations in their heads, though they seldom say them out loud:

- "I feel like my faith is under attack. Sometimes I find it hard to pray and almost impossible to make myself go to church. It's just too hard. Why can't I snap out of this funk and be the faithful Christian I desire to be?"
- "Where is God in the midst of my struggle? He doesn't seem to be hearing my prayers. Does he even understand my pain and care about me?"
- "At times God seems so far away—and I feel totally disconnected from him. It really hurts me."
- "In the past, I used to be bold and courageous in my faith, but I just don't know anymore. I'm beginning to question my faith altogether."

Do you relate to any of the negative sentiments above? Do you feel like your faith in God and sense of devotion are being attacked or eroded? If so, I want to remind you, depression is not a symptom of faithlessness, just as physical illnesses are not symptomatic of faithlessness. Christians are not exempt from their painful presence in their lives, but diseases of the mind are often harder to see and easier to hide than other types of illness, so it's time we take depression seriously before it takes more of those we love.

God certainly has the sovereign prerogative to place his heal-ing hand upon someone and totally eradicate depression from his or her life. I fully believe he possesses that kind of limitless power. But what if he chooses not to? What if that's not part of his plan for your life? What if, like in the apostle Paul's case, God decides not to remove your thorn in the flesh but instead asserts, "My grace is sufficient for you, for my strength is made perfect in weakness" (2 Cor. 12:9)? God can teach you to live with your depression faithfully and courageously. It is possible to bring glory to him in your life despite—or even through—your struggle with depression. Indeed, he may be calling you to accept your circum-stances and glorify him by setting a positive example for others in your unwavering faithfulness and Christ-like attitude.

Depression can push us to the very threshold of our psychologi-cal and spiritual limits. Our human frailty is laid bare, our complete vulnerability exposed. It requires an inordinate amount of faith and courage to survive depression's vicious onslaught. We are forced to dig deeper. To go where our faith has not yet ventured. A faithful response to depression does not necessarily entail the eradication of it, as much as it means learning to live with it without abandoning hope in the Lord. The big challenge is learning to develop a greater reliance on God in light of your struggle, trusting in His goodness, grace, and unlimited power.

§

A young woman handed the following statement to me one Sunday evening when responding to the "invitation" (or altar call) following a sermon. Her desperate, candid words speak volumes and eloquently articulate the plight of many faithful Christians who struggle with depression.

I'll just cut to the chase. I can't seem to shake this demon. Depression has been a part of my life for eleven years now, and I'm coming to terms with the idea that it may always be, in one form or another. I go back and forth in how well I handle it, but I'm starting to understand just how greatly it's shaped who I've become. In many ways it's made me strong, empathetic and full of gratitude, but all too often I'm overwhelmed with weariness, exasperation, inadequacy, and guilt. And my coping mechanism is to stop allowing myself to feel anything at all, and it hurts other people as well as myself. Please pray that I can learn to let God do what he does best and turn something empty into something full and wonderful.

Dealing with depression is neither easy nor simple. The pathway of depression is riddled with complexity and uncertainty, but it's not hopeless, so please take heart! God relentlessly pursues us. He desires a deeper and more intimate relationship with his children. But depression often sabotages our ability to appropriately respond to God's loving overtures. We must fight back!

§

Growing through Service

Depression presents us with a unique opportunity to grow by showing us the power in serving others. Investing our time, energy, skills, and resources in kingdom work is an effective way to dwell on positive and worthwhile things. While focusing on the needs of others distracts us from our own problems, it can also help us discover a clearer sense of spiritual purpose and fulfillment.

§

A Cross-Shaped Life

Standing at the epicenter of Christianity and our lives is the cross. It is the symbol that captures our hearts and draws us closer to

11

God. Its striking silhouette stands bold and upright on the horizon of time, summoning us into a more intimate relationship with our maker, redeemer, and friend. The cross is God's calling card, declaring, "I see you. I love you. I want you." It reaches out its arms to embrace the world and says, "I'm here for you." And it points upward to heaven and proclaims the Creator's care for creation.

In Christ's sacrifice upon the cross, we see not only the true depth and extent of God's loyal and unfailing commitment to us, but also the extreme measures to which he was willing to go to save us. The cross is love in action. It is love defined, and it is divine love revealed. The cross summons us, shapes us, and saves us. Furthermore, it sensitizes and mobilizes us to compassionate care.

§

The Challenge

No matter who we are as Christians, we are all fragile, broken, and imperfect earthen vessels—jars of clay. But God has chosen to use us nonetheless to carry the magnificent gospel of his amazing grace within our beings. We are commissioned to share this good news of peace and salvation with the world. Therefore, Paul writes, "We are afflicted in every way, but not crushed; perplexed, but not driven to despair; . . . struck down, but not destroyed" (2 Cor. 4:8-9). There are extremely valuable lessons we learn through suffering that can't be learned any other way.

Depression is a harsh schoolmaster, but a wise teacher when we entrust it to a loving God and acquire wisdom in living with it. God is actively working in visible and invisible ways to provide you with the necessary resources and courage to overcome and be more than a conqueror through Christ. Romans 8:37-39 states: "No, in all these things we are more than conquerors through him who loved us. For I am sure that neither death nor life, nor angels nor rulers, nor things present nor things to come, nor powers, nor height nor depth, nor anything else in all creation, will be able to separate us from the love of God in Christ

Jesus our Lord." As a believer in Christ, you can rest assured that nothing—not even the deepest depression—will ever be able to exclude you from God's love. You will never be out of his reach. No matter the circumstances, Jesus will be right there by your side helping you and strengthening your soul. In the midst of depression's dark shadow, hope is often hit hard. Therefore, you must put your trust in Christ.

Several ways depression can make you stronger include the following:

1. You can become a better problem-solver;
2. You can become better at coping with life in general;
3. You can cultivate better relationships by learning to prioritize what's most important;
4. You can become more caring and compassionate; and
5. You can become more realistic about matters of control.

Be strong and courageous, I will continue to walk alongside you on this hope-filled journey of discovery, personal growth, and healing.

§

Blue Task
#2

- Think long and hard about any potential positives related to your depression.
- Write down a list of every positive thing that has resulted from your experience of depression thus far.
- You may wish to share your list of positives on the comment section of my blog (RyanNoelFraser.com) to encourage the rest of us.

Chapter Three

☁

A Community of Care

WHEN I was growing up, it seemed that my three siblings and I couldn't get away with anything—and I mean *anything*. It was almost as if each and every parent in the neighborhood had signed a pact to keep close tabs on one another's kids. If we ever even thought about getting up to any shenanigans, generally before we ever got back home, some other adult in the community had called to inform Mom and Dad of every last detail. There was nowhere to run or hide. The jig was up!

In some ways, I wish things were still like that in our present era and that people looked out for each other and for their kids as they used to back in the good ol' days. On the rugged and untamed western frontier of North America, life was treacherous. Small groups of brave souls stuck closely together in tight-knit communities out of pure necessity. It was a matter of life and death. Everybody knew everyone else's business. Not because they were nosey, but because people needed each other's help and mutual protection as they trekked westward to stake their claim. But, sadly, times have changed. In postmodern society, our notion of "community" has morphed dramatically from what it once was.

Do you remember the Three Musketeers? Athos, Porthos, and Aramis lived by the motto, "All for one, one for all!" that was coined by their good friend, D'Artagnan (arguably the Fourth

Musketeer).[1] This inspiring and undying commitment to each other was the underlying secret to their collective strength and success. But it's hard to find that kind of loyalty and camaraderie these days isn't it—that kind of community?

§

Yet, we are reminded that our lives are inextricably interconnected, because we all have something in common: human suffering. God wants you to understand that you're not alone. Other faithful believers endure similar difficulties. We're subject to the same trials, temptations, and tribulations as unbelievers—perhaps even more so. It's an intense battle with many casualties. That's why we need each other so much.

Jesus fostered healthy relationships and spiritual connectivity wherever he went. By making himself available, the Lord made the grace of God accessible to all people, even those living on the fringes of society. But oftentimes, the depressed struggle with a pervasive sense of loneliness and isolation from others.

§

The church is portrayed in Scripture as a living organism that is intended to function as a healthy and whole interconnected body, as each of her members fulfills their respective roles (1 Cor. 12:12-31). To be a member of something far bigger than ourselves is comforting. There is strength in numbers as well as the existence of *synergy*, which is defined as follows: "The whole is greater than the sum of the parts." In other words, you can do more with less. Together we can accomplish what we

---

1   Dumas, *The Three Musketeers*, 82. Dumas, Alexandre. *The Three Musketeers*, eds. Mary Carolyn Waldrep and Suzanne E. Johnson. Unabridged version of text by George W. Jacobs and Company (Philadelphia, 1893), an English translation of *Les Trois Mousquetaires* originally published in France in 1844. Mineola, NY: Dover, 2007.

can't individually. There is a popular saying: "Together is better!" Thus, we need people in our lives. We are, indeed, better together, and we can accomplish more when we embrace those persons God has strategically placed in our lives.

The concepts of synergy and teamwork can be illustrated by "the two-horse rule." If one horse is able to pull 700 pounds and another horse 800 pounds, how much weight can they pull when harnessed together? Logically, the answer would be 1,500 pounds, but the actual answer is surprising. A two-horse team is able to pull its own weight plus the weight of their interaction. Therefore, harnessed together, the horses can pull 3,000 pounds. Other sources I researched have suggested that when horses are teamed together it is possible for them to pull up to four times the sum of what they could do by themselves. To affirm:

> Two are better than one, because they have a good return for their work: If one falls down, his friend can help him up. But pity the man who falls and has no one to help him up! Also, if two lie down together, they will keep warm. But how can one keep warm alone? Though one may be overpowered, two can defend themselves. A cord of three strands is not quickly broken. (Ecclesiastes 4:9-12 New International Version)

According to the concept of synergy, something new and exciting is created in the process of working together so that the result is greater than the sum of each individual's efforts. When we work together, the reward will always be much more satisfying.

But it is not only the reward of our work that is under consideration by Solomon; he argues that it is better for us to have a partner in difficult times. As implied in Ecclesiastes 4:12b (NIV), which says, "A cord of three strands is not quickly broken," the third strand of any strong relationship lies in a connection with our heavenly Father. This kind of spiritually bonded relationship will not dissolve easily. It will be able to withstand formidable external threats and significant pressure. To know that Christian friends "have our backs" gives us a tremendous sense of security, especially in tough times.

§

The New Testament is full of "one another" passages that clearly illustrate the above concept for us. These scriptures teach us how we ought to love one another and look out for the well-being of each other within the household of God.[2] The emotional and spiritual strength we draw from community is difficult to quantify.

When the Lord gave us the precious gift of the church, a ready-made spiritual family, he knew exactly what he was doing. Jesus recognized how important it would be for his followers to remain in solidarity and mutual loving care. The church was his divinely foreordained solution to our problem of loneliness, as well as our human need for ongoing accountability in our faith.

In times of difficulty, knowing the care of a supportive and loving church family is an indispensable resource—an amazing gift of immeasurable value. When the chips are down, the community of faith is to pull together and provide mutual care and ongoing support to one another.

Jesus taught his disciples to be about the business of serving one another and taking care of each other. At the Last Supper, Jesus demonstrated to the Twelve, through washing their feet (John 13:1-17), how they were to humbly serve others in the kingdom of heaven. The early church, under the direction of

---

2   See John 15:12, 17; Rom. 12:5, 10, 16; 13:8; 14:13; 15:5-7, 14; 16:16; 1
     Cor. 12:25-26; 16:20; 2 Cor. 13:11-12; Gal. 5:13; 6:2; Eph. 4:2, 25, 32;
     5:19, 21; Col. 3:13, 16; 1 Thess. 3:12; 4:9, 18; 5:11, 15; 2 Thess. 1:3; Heb.
     3:13; 10:24-25; James 5:16; 1 Pet. 1:22; 4:8-10; 5:5, 14; 1 John 1:7; 3:11,
     23; 4:7, 11-12; 2 John 1:5. I encourage you to carefully study these Bible
     passages to discover God's will for the community of faith.

the apostles, was united in heart and soul. They pooled all their resources together and shared their possessions with those in need, showed hospitality in their homes, and served together in humility and love (Acts 2:44-47).

As Christ's body, we must care because Jesus cared, we must share because he shared, and at times, we must place the needs of the body of Christ ahead of our own needs. There are countless ways by which we can go about strengthening our sense of community and committed service to one another and the world around us. But even within the body of Christ, we sometimes—due to depression—experience a sense of loneliness and isolation.

§

Combating Loneliness and Isolation

How do we combat loneliness and isolation? We must be proactive and can't afford to be passive in this pursuit. Though I'm not saying it's going to be easy, what follows are a few practical strategies.

The first step is to start with yourself. In other words, become your own friend. We all have an "inner child" that speaks to us throughout our lives. It can declare either words of life and encouragement or words of discouragement. We call this "self-talk." Therefore, make the conscious decision that this voice will be uplifting and positive, one that conveys to you the truth that you're special, precious to God, and worthy to be loved. Jesus tells us to love our neighbor as ourselves (Matt. 19:19), which implies self-love and self-worth. When our inner voice is constantly negative and demeaning, it produces a downward spiral of self-loathing. The things we tell ourselves *about ourselves* can be life-giving or life-sapping.

You may want to write a letter to your inner child to communicate unconditional acceptance, tender loving care, and worthiness. Here's an example written by a woman who continued to struggle with loneliness and profound loss several years after her mother's death:

> My precious Suzie,
> I am so sorry you lost your mom. The last eight years have been very hard for you. She was so much to you—your best friend, your confidant, your cheerleader, and source of unconditional love. Your mom always saw the good in you, and understood the bad. She was always just a phone call away. Now, you have been very lonely without her.
> I am going to ask you to love yourself like your mom loved you. Be your own friend. Care for yourself like your mom would and did. Hear her loving voice in your head and make it your own. The road to loving you is long, but I will be with you always.
>
> Yours always,
> Suzanne

§

Developing a healthy relationship within your self is essential for the positive seeds of self-love to take root, grow, and flourish. The next step to combatting loneliness and isolation is to pray that God will lead you to persons with whom you can develop encouraging and healthy friendships. Obviously, not all relationships are beneficial for people dealing with depression. In fact, predators and opportunists can take advantage of the weakened emotional condition of the depressed. Codependent relationships can also result in negative outcomes. Therefore, proceed cautiously and prayerfully, but don't wait indefinitely to act. Take appropriate responsibility. Do your part to seek healthy relationships that will be good for you as well as for those you befriend.

Force yourself to attend services and other church activities that will put you in direct contact with others. Seek out a trusted friend whom you are accountable to and commit to speak with them at least three times per week. Tell them upfront that depression leads you to isolate yourself from others as a means of shrinking back or hiding from the world. Ask them if they would be willing to let you call them two or three times each week so as to remain connected. If you could set up a regular weekly lunch "date" with this friend it would even be better. Just be sure that it's an appropriate relationship.

Another idea is to sign up to volunteer alongside a group of workers either at church or for a local charity or civic organization. Serving with others facilitates communication and fosters camaraderie. These strategies will push you out of your (dis) comfort zone and counteract loneliness.

§

Jesus allowed his inner being—his spirit—to be touched by the sadness and sorrow of others. He openly expressed his emotion and sadness, thereby modeling for us what "real men" and "real women" are to do. When we cry with others in their time of need, they feel like we are connecting to their pain in a meaningful manner. We are participating in their grief. Allow yourself to be vulnerable and transparent.

Jesus was driven by deep feelings of concern for others. In observing Christ's example of compassion, we see and understand more fully the Father. We are able to more clearly grasp a lucid and undistorted vision of the God who is love. The mass media has the unfortunate effect of desensitizing us to the suffering of those around us, but when we busy ourselves with the meaningful work of selflessly serving others and focusing on the needs of those around us, it helps us take our mind off our own problems.

§

Charity Begins in the Heart

When my wife, Missy, and I were young, broke college students, we discovered the meaning of "being poor and in love." We had recently moved into low-income, government-subsidized apartments and were scraping to make ends meet. Neither of us had much income to speak of and survived on our meager earnings at part-time jobs and struggled with student loans. Things were tight financially.

One late afternoon there was a knock at the door of our apartment. When I opened the door, to my shock, one of my brilliant Bible professors, Dr. Dowell Flatt, was standing outside. What was he doing at our place?

"Hello, Brother Flatt! What a big surprise! Is everything okay?"

"Ryan, everything's just fine. I'm glad I was able to locate where you and Missy live."

"Well, please won't you come inside?" I was still confused as to his presence.

"No, thanks, I just dropped by because I have something in my car for you. I heard you'd recently moved and thought you might need a few bags of groceries. Would you please accept them from me as a housewarming present?"

By now Missy was curious as to what was going on and peeked around me to see who I was talking to. "Brother Flatt? Good afternoon!"

"Hi, Missy, how are you doing?"

"I'm doing fine. I'm just surprised to see you," she said.

"I imagine that's true," replied Dr. Flatt. "I was just telling Ryan that I bought a couple of bags of groceries for you guys."

"Really? That is so kind of you . . ." Missy's voice cracked. "I don't know what to say."

"You don't need to say anything. Just accept them as a small token of love from my wife Della and me."

We were deeply touched. I could hardly believe it. Not only had Brother Flatt taken the time and trouble to find out where we lived, but he'd seen a real need and had responded in a tangible way. I followed him out to his car where he popped the trunk. I helped him carry into our apartment three or four grocery bags containing basics like milk, eggs, bread, sandwich meat, and some canned foods. We placed them on the kitchen table.

Before departing, he said, "I just wanted you both to know that I care about you and wanted to help you, especially since you're both living a long distance from your families."

All we could say was "Thank you! We really appreciate it."

Dr. Flatt didn't stay long, but he made a huge impression on us. We'll never forget that one simple act of kindness. No strings attached. No hidden agenda, except perhaps the sense of personal satisfaction that comes from doing a good deed. In that moment, this humble, godly man powerfully demonstrated for us the meaning of Christian charity.

We learned years later, after his untimely death, that Dr. Dowell Flatt had severely suffered with clinical depression most of his adult life.

§

In Scripture, the concept of charity is prevalent within the contexts of both Israel and the church. The people of God were commanded to care for the vulnerable populations living among them. In this era, the church is charged with the God-given responsibility of ethical, charitable care for those who are in need. Within our families, friendship, churches, communities, and the larger world there are countless opportunities to follow in Jesus's footsteps of humble servitude. We can discover a clearer sense of spiritual purpose and find personal life fulfillment in service to others. James 1:27 (ESV) says, "Religion that is pure and undefiled before God, the Father, is this: to visit orphans and widows in their affliction, and to keep oneself unstained from the world." Because of God's heart for the poor, he expects the body of Christ to take appropriate measures in its responsiveness.

Charity begins at home. Within physical families, it is our obligation to take care of our own immediate relatives. Galatians 6:10 (ESV), however, also exhorts, "So then, as we have opportunity, let us do good to everyone, and especially to those who are of the household of faith." Unique situations occasionally arise in which the church is called upon to supply various material needs (i.e., food, clothing, shelter, transportation, medical expenses, utility bills, etc.). Jesus proclaimed, "It is more blessed to give than to receive" (Acts 20:35, ESV). However, there is a way to go about it and a way not to do it. The body of Christ is called to be a community of care. The principles taught in the New Testament regarding how charity should be performed include the following:

1. anonymity so as to bring glory to God rather than ourselves (Matt. 6:2-4);
2. humility (Luke 14:12-14);
3. faithful sincerity (James 2:15-17); and
4. sacrificial love (1 Cor. 13).

§

Blue Task
#3

- Write a letter of compassion to your inner child expressing love and concern for yourself.
- Pray for your inner child.
- Find somebody who seems to be struggling whom you can minister to and serve this week. Make a concrete plan on how you will try and reach out to them in the next few days to infuse some compassionate love and kindness into their lives. Perhaps you could bake something delicious for someone, rake a person's leaves, clean out their gutters, or tune up their car.

Chapter Four

The Ministry of
Presence

WHEN the going gets rough, we typically find out who our
real friends are. These are not the fair-weather friends that seem
to vanish into thin air the instant the storms of life overwhelm
us. Fair-weather friends are "a dime a dozen." True friends are
few and far between.

Jesus modeled for his disciples how to be a true friend. The
Jewish religious leaders often criticized him for the type of company
he chose to keep but for Christ, companionship was always a
means to an end, never an end in and of itself. He had an eternal
spiritual purpose for it, in that it served as a vehicle whereby he
built connections to individuals in order to draw them closer to
God. Christ's incarnation is used as the springboard to commend a
ministry of presence (i.e., being there for others).

§

Conversation as a Gift

To listen well is to show that we care. People crave to be heard
and understood by others. It means that they matter at least to
one other person. People also need to be approached in a manner
that touches the deeper realms of their existence, namely their
souls. Most persons in this lost and dying world are starving for

spiritually meaningful conversation, that which reaches beneath the surface of their humanity, fostering personal growth and eternal hope. Our conversations ought to be baptized in themes of Christian faith and spiritual life, including worship, ministry, and our experience of God's presence in our lives. When we hear people speak of their various struggles, we need to be ready to explore with them where God is in all the confusion and chaos, and refer them to qualified help if you sense the need.

§

Making Contact

I'm passionate about pastoral care and ministry because I'm passionate about people. I care deeply about those that suffer and want to comfort them. I also desire to equip others to gain confidence and the needed skills to reach out with God's love because I myself have experienced deep sympathy from others. When I was sixteen years old, a freak gymnastic accident resulted in a serious neck injury. I could have become paralyzed. During my frightening ordeal, many people came to my aid and showed me love and support. Through a long recovery, I was nursed back to health and now know what it's like to be vulnerable and on the receiving end of care. The outpouring of compassion I received from others touched me deeply and was the impetus for my becoming more sensitive to the needs of others. It opened my eyes and made me want to reach out.

§

A Life-Changing Experience
This is how my story unfolded.

As the son of missionaries living in Cape Town, South Africa, I attended a public school. One day in gym class, Mr. Wright divided us boys into groups to perform various gymnastic elements. We rotated among stations such as climbing a rope, vaulting, using the pommel horse, and gymnastic rings. Our group had moved to a station where we were to do a back handspring. Mr. Wright asked me to demonstrate for the class. I took my position standing up on the wooden gymnastics bench, about fourteen inches off the floor with my back toward the mat. My friends, Graham Morton and Gavin Greenwood, flanked me on either side. Their job was to help me flip over. I leaned forward, coiling my body to spring backward, but as I flung my arms back, my left elbow struck Gavin's head. He couldn't hold on and both spotters let go of me. My body turned upside down—and I landed on my head.

An electric shock traveled through my nervous system. I lay motionless, unable to move my arms or legs. I grimaced in agony because of the excruciating pain. Mr. Wright rushed over and classmates gathered around while keeping a safe distance. After a phone call, my father was there in minutes. He burst through the large wooden double doors and we soon heard sirens blaring as an ambulance arrived not many minutes later. Two EMTs rushed in and evaluated me. With an attentive tone in his voice, one asked, "Where are you hurting? Can you wiggle your toes?" I did my best to answer his questions as they secured my neck in a brace and carefully lifted me onto the gurney. Next, they wheeled me outdoors. A warm gentle breeze set my left arm ablaze. The pain was indescribable. Fear and confusion filled my mind. Terrifying thoughts raced through my head.

What's wrong with my body? Am I going to be permanently paralyzed?

The EMTs wheeled me down the sidewalk and loaded me into the ambulance. Students and teachers looked on in alarm. The fifteen-minute trip to the Tygerberg Hospital—the second largest medical center in South Africa—was a bumpy ride. The gurney I was lying on rattled and shifted every time we hit a pothole or took a sharp corner. Pain like a lightning bolt shot through my arm with each jolt.

On arrival, a couple of ER nurses wheeled me into radiology. The X-rays revealed I had broken my C-3 and C-4 vertebrae in my neck, having shattered the fourth. Scary scenarios ran through my head.

Will I ever recover?

A team of specialists gathered around as the senior doctor leaned toward me. "Do you want to hear the good news or the bad news first?" he asked with a droll smile.

"Please tell me the good news first."

"You're a lucky young man. The C-4 fracture was a couple of millimeters from rendering you paralyzed for life. But your prognosis for a full recovery is good."

These words came as a giant relief. But I knew there was more he wasn't saying.

"So, what's the bad news?" I asked.

He furrowed his brow and displayed sincere concern.

"You'll be in traction—flat on your back—for six weeks. We've got to drill holes into the sides of your head slightly above your ears to screw bolts into your skull. We'll attach them to a caliper. The apparatus will then be connected to a cable on a pulley system with weights hanging at the end of it. Your neck needs to be stretched out while your broken vertebrae heal."

Tears welled up in my eyes.

Less than an hour after the accident, my ability to move three of my limbs returned—except for my left arm. That would take forty-eight hours. My stay in the hospital ended up lasting two months due to the development of kidney stones caused by my sedentary condition. Those had to be surgically removed, leaving a thirteen-inch scar on my left side.

§

While in the hospital, I felt helpless—at the mercy of medical personnel. To be that needy, exposed, and vulnerable was embarrassing and made me uncomfortable and self-conscious. They fed me, bathed me, changed me, and sterilized my head wounds, applying a yellow goop to my drilled-head incisions daily. Here I was, a fit and athletic sixteen-year-old boy, now feeling like a helpless baby. Nurses rigged up mirrors on a metal contraption above me and behind my head, so I could look around the room and watch TV. They provided a clear acrylic podium so I could place books upside down on the see-through surface a couple of feet above my face to read. Holding them in my hands for extended periods turned out to be exhausting. But on the podium, I only touched a book when turning the page. Nurses positioned plates of food on my chest and I used the overhead mirrors so I could see to guide a knife, fork, or spoon to my mouth. It was tricky and took some getting used to. My prolonged time in traction produced bedsores on the back of my head causing clumps of hair to fall out. My scalp became raw and terribly sensitive. It hurt constantly and seeped a sticky substance—blood plasma. A foam donut went under my head to relieve some of the pain.

§

While I was laid up, people visited me to help pass the time. I was thankful for their caring spirits and genuine concern. I never felt forgotten or abandoned.

Friends caught me up on all the latest news of what was going on back at school or church. They cracked jokes and engaged me in light conversation. At times, things got a bit awkward when visitors ran out of things to say. When they were about to leave, the last thing they would often ask would be something like "Is there anything I can do for you? Do you need anything?" They meant well but felt powerless to fix my situation.

My parents and two younger sisters brought me the Lord's Supper on Sundays. In our church we observe this sacrament every week. Therefore, it meant a lot to me to be afforded the opportunity to participate in it regularly while I was hospitalized. We shared a short devotional together including a scripture, song, and prayer. These simple religious rituals helped me feel connected to God.

As the weeks passed, my eye sockets appeared sunken, as my face grew gaunt. My muscles gradually atrophied. So much so, that when I was released from the hospital, I had to relearn how to walk. My body had little strength. It felt like I had turned into a feeble old man, but my hope for recovery remained. I sensed God's abiding presence.

§

With excitement in her voice, a nurse finally announced, "It's time for you to go home. Are you ready?" What a question! The prospect filled me with jubilance. The joy flooding through me was so overwhelming that if I hadn't been so weak, I would have jumped up and danced my way down the corridor. Obviously, that wasn't possible, so the nurse escorted me in a wheelchair to the main hospital door instead. Dad met us there and helped me climb into the car. He was all smiles. Although it was a rainy day, my spirit was bright.

My mom and sisters were anxiously awaiting my arrival. Mom had prepared an elaborate roast beef dinner to celebrate my homecoming. They had decorated my bedroom with a Welcome Home sign and streamers. It felt wonderful to be home again. Being back in my own bed with familiar surroundings gave me a sense of peace. I lay there with my head propped up and basked in the sunlight as it filtered through my window. My room had the comfort of sameness, but I was different.

My post-hospital recovery lasted several months. At first, I had to wear a rigid plastic neck and upper body ("cervical-thoracic orthopedic") brace. The discomfort rubbed my chin raw. Friends popped in to cheer me up. They brought me crossword puzzles and yummy snacks. But most of all, they listened to me as I told my story. I had biweekly visits to a physical therapist's home to teach me exercises to stretch and strengthen my muscles. Tutors helped me catch up with schoolwork I had missed. My friend Gavin, a math wiz, gave me trigonometry lessons. Over the next few months, I healed physically and emotionally. I still needed ongoing assistance from others and relied on their sympathetic support and expertise. Those experiences helped.

§

Many years have passed since that painful ordeal and today I enjoy good health, yet I cannot forget the people who visited me in the hospital and at home during one of my life's most critical and desperate periods. Today, I would call that a "ministry of presence." Just by being there for me they provided comfort and encouragement.

That profound experience shaped my perspective on God and my life's purpose. It also enlarged my capacity for empathy and increased my ability to display compassion toward others. Had the accident not happened, I might not have decided during my senior year of high school to pursue a career in the ministry. I believe that God spared me from paralysis and healed me to open me to the positives of pain—my own and the pain of others. I'd like you to ponder the five questions below:

1. Have you gone through a personally life-transforming experience?
2. Have you observed kindhearted and compassionate care in action?
3. Have you been negatively impacted by an absence of care?
4. Have these experiences made you more aware of

    people's needs and motivated you to make a positive
    difference in their lives?

5.   Do you want to become a more skillful caregiver?

§

All around us, individuals are hurting. We see evidence of suffering. Within our own families, churches, schools, workplaces, and communities people need loving care.

They need *your* loving care.

If you're encouraged to be God's hands in this world, you're not alone. Many believers seek to care for others effectively. You can become a more competent and compassionate caregiver, but it's hard to know where to begin. I learned a great deal about compassion, because I received it, but another important resource for me has been the Bible, where I read of God's care for His creation. Reading Scripture in a systematic and guided way took on new meaning after my accident and recovery.

The Son of God's deep commitment to care and offer his healing touch to others has taught me how to apply important caregiving principles from God's Word to the attitudes and actions I take toward those in need. Scripture reveals many instances in which Jesus interacted directly with suffering people. Those individuals came from diverse backgrounds and struggled with physical, emotional, relational, and spiritual ailments. Their stories remain relevant to me. They connect with me on the most basic human level and challenge me to be more merciful and heighten my awareness of my responsibility to lovingly serve others. I'm moved by Christ's compassionate care of those individuals he came into contact with who were suffering. It opens my spiritual eyes to new and exciting possibilities for meaningful, Christ-centered service.

§

Suggested Ways to Be Present

Some proactive steps you may want to consider when it comes to being present (or "making contact" with) those who are hurting include the following:

1. Write a card to a shut-in, new mother, someone recovering from surgery, or an individual who has lost a loved one or a beloved pet.
2. Make encouraging phone calls to those you are aware of who are struggling in their lives.
3. Develop a prayer list, which includes the names of specific individuals whom you want to lift up to God on a regular basis.

§

Have you ever been visiting with an older person and gotten "caught in conversation?" The familiar story they launch into, recounting every last detail, is one you've heard them tell numerous times before. There you sit politely, trying your best to look interested, but in all honesty you feel trapped.

As a minister, I've often found myself in situations like this while visiting with the elderly at nursing homes. As a college professor, there have also been occasions I've been hard-pressed for time when students have caught me after class or stopped by my office unannounced to talk. These days, I'm wary when anyone says to me, "Do you have a quick minute?" because it usually entails more than one. However, there's one thing for sure, and that is this: the importance and value of being a good listener cannot be overstated.

To listen well is to show that we care by giving others a few minutes of our time. Those deemed to be the best conversationalists are usually, not surprisingly, also the best listeners. Being someone who is approachable and shows genuine interest in what others have to say—no matter how trivial their words may seem to be on the surface—is of immeasurable value. How does the old saying go? "God gave us two ears and only one mouth, so we ought to listen twice as much as we speak."

§

What made Jesus such an amazingly effective conversationalist? How did he model spiritual care though his distinctive style of interpersonal communication? First of all, he was clearly a skilled reflective listener. He intuitively knew how to draw people out of themselves by his extraordinary listening ability. Even as a twelve-year-old, Jesus demonstrated the uncanny ability to listen and relate well to others, often to those far older than himself. In Luke 2:41-47, we read of an occasion when Jesus's parents made a pilgrimage to Jerusalem to celebrate the Passover Feast. When the family returned home with a large group of travelers from Nazareth, Joseph and Mary left Jesus behind by mistake. I have often wondered what terrifying thoughts must have crossed their minds: *What are we going to do? We have literally lost the Son of God!* (Wouldn't you have loved to eavesdrop on that conversation?) They simply had no idea where he was, so they returned to Jerusalem to search. After three days, they finally went looking for him in the temple complex—or perhaps they went there to pray that God would lead them to His Son. To their great relief they found Jesus in the temple courts. What was he doing there? The Bible says he was "sitting among the teachers, listening to them and asking them questions. Everyone who heard him was amazed at his understanding and his answers" (Luke 2:46-47, NIV).

It may be inferred that Jesus's idea of being about his heavenly Father's business was entering into conversation with others concerning spiritual matters. Jesus was not just idly passing the time by hanging out and shooting the breeze. His conversations, even from this young age, were packed with weighty content and spiritual poignancy. He knew precisely what questions to ask to evoke the theological imagination of others, and he knew how to respond to questions wisely, with words *seasoned with spiritual salt and grace* (Col. 4:6). People felt affirmed when talking with him because he paid close attention to their deepest longings and concerns. Jesus also possessed the uncanny ability to ask penetrating and thought-provoking questions that stirred up a person's soulful yearnings.

§

On a scale of one to ten, how do your conversations measure up to the Jesus standard? Do you tend to stay in shallow, safe water or do you take your conversations to a deeper level that holds spiritual significance? In our North American culture, we are notorious for squandering the bulk of our time and energy on that which is temporal, shallow, and inconsequential. We generally fail to focus on the most vital things of this life and the eternal existence to come. People have many masks they hide behind. Regrettably, we're more likely to be complicit in this pointless charade than dare to ask the more penetrating questions that delve into matters of true importance. We do this because to stay shallow is to play it safe.

Jesus didn't play it safe. He took calculated risks to cut through the facades of people's floundering spiritual lives. In Matthew 16:13-20, Jesus travels to the region of Caesarea Philippi with his disciples. Without prior warning he poses a poignant question, "Who do people say the Son of Man is?" (v. 13b, NIV). The disciples respond variously with a few of the popular opinions about Jesus that are beginning to circulate. They tell Jesus that some people are speculating that he is perhaps the re-embodiment of certain famous, fiery prophets such as John the Baptist or Elijah or perhaps Jeremiah. This is, of course, all hearsay.

Jesus could have conveniently chosen to cease probing his disciples at this point in the conversation. He could have said something benign like, "That's interesting. I was just curious to hear what people out there are saying about me." But he doesn't. He gets up close and personal with them: "But what about you? . . . Who do you say I am?" (v. 15, NIV). This is what really matters. Everything in their lives hinges on how they answer this question. Their view concerning his identity is of ultimate importance to the course of their lives and future ministry; moreover, to their eternal salvation.

This conversation provides an opportunity for the disciples to look deep within their own hearts and perform a reality check, a self-assessment of their current level of faith and trust in Jesus. Simon Peter is the first to break the silence. He declares, "You are the Christ, the Son of the living God" (v. 16, NIV). Jesus does not need to hear this confession of faith for his own edification. However, Peter and the other disciples need to hear Peter say it out loud. The idea has been marinating for some time, but now it's time for it to really sink in. This "good confession" will be the litmus test of their faith and for all Christian believers to come in the future.

When we name it, we claim it! By Peter's voicing of his deepest inner thoughts, his faith suddenly became all the more real both to him and to his companions. His bold statement couldn't be taken back. But notice how Jesus had to draw it out of him. It took some intentional exploring and challenging to elicit this type of faithful response. What was once *implicit* had now become *explicit*. What was once private and hidden was now a public declaration of loyalty and devotion. What had till recently been a personally held belief now became a public profession of faith in Jesus Christ.

Jesus went on to affirm and expound upon Peter's confession of faith, indicating that the church would ultimately be established upon this rock-solid truth and that the gates of Hades would never overcome it. Jesus then ordained spiritual authority for Peter and the other disciples for their upcoming Christian mission to the world. What an intensely powerful and spiritually transformative conversation! Jesus was preparing his disciples for bold and courageous service in the kingdom of God. These men needed to know with certainty where they stood, what they believed, and the One in whom they trusted.

§

How often are we given the opportunity to make a big difference in the life of another person, but our conversation somehow misses the mark and falls miserably short? We're self-conscious about our own struggles and feel hypocritical and ineligible to serve as an ambassador for Christ because of it. This factor represents a major roadblock when it comes to personal evangelism (sharing the good news of Jesus) and genuine openness in our level of transparency or self-disclosure. We shrink back from sharing our own story of suffering as it relates to our relationship with the Lord for fear of being judged unfairly. Therefore, we stick to the surface stuff and never begin to mine the depths of the Spirit. The temporal overshadows the eternal, so we fail to ask the important questions. We cower away from meaningful conversation in order to stay in safe and predictable territory. We talk about the weather, the game, the latest movie, fashion, politics, vacation plans, school, work, family, and even church activities—the list goes on and on. But the one topic we shy away from is clearly the most important thing—our relationship with Jesus Christ and what he means in our life.

In avoiding this topic, we squander the opportunity to ask others what difference Jesus is making in their lives. We also circumvent questions that matter the most, such as "How have you and God been getting along lately? What is God doing in your life right now, and how are you answering his call to a deeper faith?" Instead, we beat around the bush and avoid God-talk altogether. Again, I believe that often behind this tendency in depressed persons with regard to spiritual conversations is the self-defeating belief that their disease automatically disqualifies them from sharing their faith. It feels threatening, even terrifying, to speak openly and honestly about one's own struggle with depression as it relates to one's walk with God.

Come to think of it, we ironically feel guilty of this in church settings. The one place in this world we should feel free to be candid about our faith struggles, we instead talk about everything under the sun, except the Son. We wonder to ourselves, *who am I to say anything? What qualifies me to share my faith or initiate talking about the Lord with anybody at all?* This internal tension holds us back and prevents us from being bold for Christ in our day-to-day interactions with others. The apostle Paul challenges, "For God did not give us a spirit of timidity, but a spirit of power, of love and of self-discipline. So, do not be ashamed to testify about our Lord" (2 Tim. 1:7-8a, NIV). We are called to be courageous in our Christian witness. Mature love for the Lord and genuine concern for others casts out our counterproductive doubts and insecurities surrounding depression. Yes, the devil desires to diminish, dismantle, and defeat God's efforts through us. Ask God to fine-tune your spiritual radar to look for opportunities for the Holy Spirit to work in and speak through you. When you hear people discuss their various struggles, consider opening up to share your own personal testimony of your struggles with the blues. This may open the door to exploring with them where God is in all the chaos of their lives. How do they sense God's abiding presence? What might they do to seek God's presence with greater intentionality? What wisdom may they glean from Scripture to inform their decision-making or find comfort and strength through their personal struggles? How may they respond more faithfully to life's challenges in such a way that God is glorified?

As our conversations focus on Jesus, our connections to the Father and to one another deepen and our conversations count for something worthwhile. Ask God to help you be bolder in raising spiritual issues in your casual conversations. Let God turn your weakness and vulnerability into strength and courage.

§

Salt-Seasoned Speech

Paul says, "Be wise in the way you act toward outsiders; make the most of every opportunity. Let your conversation be always full of grace, seasoned with salt, so that you may know how to answer everyone" (Colossians 4:5-6, NIV). These two verses are packed with godly wisdom as well as Christian challenge. We are instructed to be careful in the way we interact with outsiders (or non-Christians), so as to actively seek opportunities to share the healing and hope-filled message of the gospel of Christ in a palatable way.

For our conversations to always be *full of grace* speaks to the content of what we say as well as the manner in which we say it, namely being *grace-full* in our tone and language. For our conversations to be *seasoned with salt* implies them having some of the unique qualities of salt, with the preservation of hope and faith in God's love and power. Salt *flavors* and *seasons* food, just like our conversations can bring spiritual flavor to the bitter and bland world surrounding us, so that the gospel message can effect healing and spiritual wholeness in the lives of others.

In other words, our verbal interactions with others are a powerful means to touch their souls with the grace and mercy of God. Through our *salty and savoring speech,* we are empowered to become vessels of God's grace, as in jars of clay (2 Cor. 4:7), to those we come in contact with who are struggling and suffering.

§

A few years ago, while waiting in line at a restaurant near my university office, I spotted a colleague whom I hadn't spoken to in a while. I happened to know that this particular individual was struggling with a debilitating chronic disease. After briefly reintroducing myself to her, I infused the conversation with some deeper spiritual meaning. "I know you've been going through some tough times recently, but I am confident that

God will see you through." One sentence was all I spoke. That was the sum total of it. However, she reacted as if I had just injected a stout dose of spiritual medicine into her soul. Her face immediately lit up. With a sparkle in her eyes she said, "That's right, with God's help, I'm going to make it through!"

I gently smiled and assured her that she would remain in my prayers. This entire verbal exchange occurred in less than forty-five seconds, but I believe that there was spiritual power in it. It doesn't have to be a lengthy, drawn-out conversation, it just requires awareness and spiritual sensitivity on our part to give oomph to our words. Who knows what type of impact our spirit-led words might have in the life of a struggling sojourner?

You may have already noticed from Scripture that Jesus's interchanges with others were often brief, yet extremely meaningful and packed a powerful punch. Christ-centered conversation is about bringing hope, comfort, and reconciled identity. It can facilitate transformation to the emotionally bogged down, a freedom that only Christ can bring into someone's life.

§

Talking on the Road to Emmaus

Luke 24:13-35 speaks of the disciples traveling on the road to Emmaus, immediately following Christ's resurrection. As Cleopas and his unnamed companion discuss the tragic events of the crucifixion and perplexing post-resurrection happenings, Jesus meets them in disguised form and walks along with them. The pattern of the ensuing conversation is enlightening.

Once more, Jesus models for us the care of spirit-led conversation. Initially he asks some relevant questions, such as "What are you discussing together as you walk along?" (v. 17, NIV) and regarding the recent happenings, "What things?" (v. 19) and in so doing, Jesus demonstrates to us how to listen reflectively and give others the space to tell their stories (vv. 18-24). He takes a "not knowing" position to allow these two disciples the opportunity to unload their grief and disappointment regarding the crucifixion of their friend.

People need to feel heard, understood, and appreciated before being willing to listen to what we may want to share with them. After Jesus takes time to patiently listen to their story, he proceeds to unfold the truth to these two confused and despairing men (vv. 25-27). Craving more insights, the disciples insist that Jesus stay the night with them. It is only in the breaking of bread at suppertime that their eyes are finally opened to his true identity. Jesus immediately disappears from their sight.

Luke 24:32 (NIV) recounts, "They asked each other, 'Were not our hearts burning within us while he talked with us on the road and opened the Scriptures to us?'" Their hearts had been deeply touched by the rich and meaningful spiritual conversation they had shared with the Lord. The conversation had re-enlivened their souls and reawakened their faith.

When we converse with others, through the means of our compassionate attending, and reflective listening, their hearts may also *burn within them* as they are touched deeply by the grace and healing power of God's love residing in us. People's souls crave conversations that probe deeper levels of spirituality. We all too often waste our time "shooting the breeze" rather than "sharing the Spirit." Those suffering individuals we encounter need their souls to be touched and ministered to, just as we do.

In the biblical examples we have discussed, Jesus initiated the conversation with a couple of soul-searching questions, then listened before he leaped in. Depending on the types of initial responses he received, Jesus used their statements to shape the direction in which he went with them.

A word of caution may be in order here: some persons are not yet ready or primed for deeper levels of communication, and to impose (or force) a spiritual conversation with such people may result in unintended damage. Spiritual conversation can be a powerful means of reaching out to the lonely, hurting, and lost, but we need to show respect and exercise wisdom in the process.

§

Dear God,
Please give us the right words to say, at the right time and in the right way, to those suffering individuals we come into contact with. Empower us to share your love and mercy. Give us the courage and wisdom to find our voices so that we might be your mouthpieces to persons in need of care. Let us be humble servants and may our words always be seasoned with salt and full of grace.

In Jesus's name, Amen.

§

Blue Task
#4

- Make plans to visit someone who is in the hospital, a nursing home, or jail. Prior to visiting, pray that God will reach out to the person in such a way that they realize you and God have not forgotten about them.
- Make appropriate preparations for the visit. If possible, make or purchase a small gift to take to the individual. (Most people appreciate thoughtful gifts).
- Find a couple of uplifting and comforting passages of Scripture that you may be able to share with the individual to bring divine encouragement.
- If appropriate, during the visit you may ask permission to say a prayer for the person.

Chapter Five

Drowning in Depression

WHEN depression hits us hard, it hurts. Deeply.

I've battled with sporadic bouts of melancholy. My wife Missy, however, has struggled much more than I have, especially during the past decade. This acute difficulty has been due to the cumulative effect of genetics, a severely sick son, losing her mother, a kidney transplant, plus numerous other personal and family stressors. She has taught me quite a bit about what it's like to live with depression.

I've also observed that believers living with depression often feel guilty for their dispiritedness. They assume personal responsibility as if they've brought this struggle upon themselves. Many mull over in their minds and/or state out loud, "If only I had more faith, I wouldn't struggle with depression the way I do." They are highly self-judgmental and hypercritical as if they're somehow spiritually deficient. While they offer grace and sympathetic understanding to others, they struggle to extend it to themselves. We're often pretty good at beating ourselves up when we feel unworthy and useless.

Others feel like they're drowning in the sea of despair that frequently accompanies depression. They feel powerless to combat their emotional difficulties, resulting in a profound sense of hopelessness. To them their future looks bleak. Do you or someone you know relate to any of these perspectives or sentiments?

I want to help you in your battle with depression, but I can't promise you the complete eradication of gloom. To do so would not only be reckless, but also unethical, untrue, and unrealistic. We'd have to be dead or emotionally stunted not to feel sadness and melancholy once in a while. Let's face it: life is just plain hard and unfair at times. In fact, Jesus once said to his disciples, "I have told you these things, so that in me you may have peace. In this world you will have trouble. But take heart! I have overcome the world" (John 16:33, NIV). His jarring yet truthful words served as a reality check to the Twelve just as they do to believers today.

§

Back in my youth-ministry days in the early nineties, I served a church in Bartlesville, Oklahoma. Toward the end of the summer, I took twelfth graders on a leadership retreat called "Senior Summit" held at a beautiful, rustic facility near Branson, Missouri, on Table Rock Lake. We hired a pontoon boat and took the students out on the water for a memorable lesson called, "Get in the boat!"

After the teaching session was over, we piloted the vessel over to some spectacular forty-foot bluffs where thrill-seekers were leaping off into the lake. Approximately ten other boats had cast anchor in the deep blue water about seventy-five yards from the shoreline. Some of the kids in our group were daredevils—or at least pretended to be—and wanted to jump off the cliffs. I wasn't about to let them show me up. We dived overboard and swam toward the one and only place where it was possible to climb up some rocks onto the shore. Because several other individuals had the same idea, there was a waiting line in the lake stacked five to seven people deep, all waiting their turn to climb up onto the bank and scale the bluffs. One of the young men in our group, Nathan, floated in front of me. He was a skinny, lanky boy with jet-black hair and dark brown eyes. He'd surprised me by his gutsy—if not rash—decision to rise up to the challenge. Nathan wasn't a good swimmer. He wore himself out trying to make his way over to the shore. We must have been in water at least thirty feet deep. A few other individuals were treading water in line in front of him. By the time he got close to the climb-out point, he began to panic and flounder. Nathan swallowed water and started sinking. I frog-dived into the murky water and managed to pull him back to the surface and push him up onto the rocks. He was sputtering and gasping for breath. His eyes were dilated. My heart raced with anxiety. How would I have broken the news to his parents that their oldest son had drowned under my watch?

Perhaps you too are sinking, not like Nathan, but under the pull of your pain, problems, or pressures. Perhaps you or a loved one is drowning emotionally. You feel helpless, hopeless, and horrified. I'd like to reach out and grab you. I don't want you to drown but to live life to the fullest. God does, too.

§

I told you the story about a boy who was literally drowning. Now, here's an example of a woman who was emotionally drowning. I'll call her Emily.

Emily sat pensively across from me in my counseling office. By all appearances, this thirty-something successful business-woman seemed exhausted and frazzled. Mascara marks stained both cheeks. The skin on her face and neck was blotchy.

"Emily, how may I help you today?"

She made brief eye contact and then stared out the window. She seemed to be lost in thought. She struggled to speak, but evidently couldn't find the words.

After a prolonged silence I asked, "What's on your mind?"

She furrowed her brow and shook her head as if frustrated with herself and her lip began to quiver. Finally, she blurted out "I feel like I'm drowning!" Tears filled her eyes.

"Tell me more."

Emily sniffled and shrugged. She lowered her head and stared at the carpet for a moment. "It's like I'm sinking and can't breathe. I'm going down deeper and deeper into dark waters."

I leaned forward. "What do you mean by sinking?"

"I feel like the harder I try to swim my way back to the surface, I've got weights tied to my ankles and sink back down."

The tone of her voice sounded desperate. Hopeless.

Emily started sobbing. I waited for her to regain her composure, then I gently encouraged her to share a bit more of her story.

She reached for a tissue in the box on my coffee table and dabbed her eyes and blew her nose. "I'm sorry."

"I don't mind tears."

"Sometimes it seems like I'll never recover . . . never get back to the surface."

"Sounds painful and frightening . . . your hope is slipping away."

She nodded. "It is. It's felt that way for a while now."

"Maybe—with God's help—we can do something about that together."

Coming to me for counseling was Emily's way of crying for help.

And you may be an Emily. Few people understand how life is for you—how challenging every day is. How isolated you feel. Even the tasks of getting out of bed in the morning, showering, dressing, preparing breakfast, and driving to work seem like insurmountable struggles.

§

Though I can't fully relate to the depth of Emily's abasement, I do connect in some ways. There have been periods in my life when I've felt something like that. I cried for no apparent reason. The experience of these disquieting emotions sapped my energy. They also tainted my perspective and negatively affected my attitude. I didn't like the way I felt, but at the time felt powerless to do anything about my state of mind. If I were to label my experience, I would call it periodic or situational depression.

From experience, I know the heavy toll that melancholia takes, but my Missy has struggled with a more serious depressive disorder for a number of years. Her mother, as well as her maternal grandmother, also had personal difficulties with forlornness, so Missy was perhaps genetically predisposed to it. The trigger for her was the cumulative effect of stress and grief related to moving far away from her Kansas home, and our youngest son being diagnosed with leukemia. Immediately I think of Missy's mom passing away during this time. Then Missy required a kidney transplant in 2007 due to renal failure and resigned from her job a few months later. The accumulation of things added up to an unbearable situation for her that overwhelmed her coping mechanisms.

About three months after Missy's kidney transplant, her nephrologist[3] at Vanderbilt, Dr. Heidi Schaefer, asked Missy if she had any questions at the end of her office visit. Missy said, "Yes, just one. Why am I not happy? One of my best friends in the world just gave me his kidney, my husband is faithful to me, and we are blessed with two beautiful children, Olivia and Austin. I feel so guilty for being depressed. What is wrong with me?" What Dr. Heidi said next continues to help Missy daily deal with this disease. She caringly touched Missy's shoulder and said, "That's exactly what depression is. It doesn't make sense. You have it and it's real. Please let me help you." She probably doesn't realize it, but Dr. Heidi changed all of our lives that day. She did more than any physician had done previously. Dr. Heidi reached out in compassionate care and

---

3   A nephrologist is an MD who specializes in kidney (or renal) care.

understanding. My wife had tried to combat her despondency without medication as long as she could. She finally realized, with her wonderful physician's sage counsel, that she needed to start taking antidepressants to help her cope more effectively. I'm proud of how well she has managed and her courageous acceptance of the realities and limitations resulting from her depressive disorder.

§

My purpose here is partly to remind you of a divine reality beyond your disease or present malaise. Here it is: God loves you. He always has; He's never stopped. He always will. He completely understands what you're going through and cares about you and your situation deeply. Psalm 34:18 (ESV) says, "The Lord is near to the brokenhearted and saves the crushed in spirit." Psalm 147:3 assures us that "He heals the brokenhearted and binds up their wounds." Though it may feel to you that God is a million miles away, He is not. He is right there with you, right now. He is holding your hand and won't ever let go of you as He lovingly leads you through the valley of the shadow of death (Psa. 23:4a), is holding you, protecting you, and comforting you along your fear-provoking path of suffering (v. 4b). He will see you through, come what may. It may not feel like it to you, but it's true!

There's another piece to what I want to say to you. Please bear with me for a moment. One of the most powerful and effective strategies to combat the darkness of depression and black abyss of grief is to look beyond yourself, if only for a few minutes, and find a way to serve others. I'm not necessarily saying it's an easy thing to do; but it can be extremely helpful. Performing small acts of kindness by reaching out to others with God's love reminds us of our own God-imaged nature and identity, including our inherent worth. It also serves as a good distraction—even if only a momentary escape—from our personal pain and suffering. When we selflessly serve others, in return we receive a sense of genuine purpose, Christ-centered hope, and spiritual joy. Matthew 20:28 (ESV) reveals something rather profound and potent to us, that "the Son of man came not to be served but to serve, and to give his life as a ransom for many." There is life-changing meaning and a transformative sense of purpose, eternal hope, and unparalleled joy in service, so if you're dealing with a bad case of the blues, think of practical and tangible ways that you might challenge yourself to step out of your (dis)comfort zone to make a positive difference in the lives of others. It doesn't have to be some grand gesture—just something thoughtful, kind, and considerate. By doing so you will demonstrate to yourself and to those around you what you're really made of: namely compassion, generosity of spirit, and Christian goodness.

Jesus once said, "It is more blessed to give than to receive" (Acts 2:35, ESV). He was right. The true blessing in being a generous and humble servant ultimately belongs to us, because we will reap what we sow. Galatians 6:9 (ESV) says, "And let us not grow weary of doing good, for in due season we will reap, if we do not give up." Think of tangible ways that you may be able to reach out to someone who is drowning emotionally with overwhelming life stress, anxiety, sorrow, or depression. What would represent a lifeline you may be able to toss to them? Lifelines come in many shapes and forms. Sometimes they may be a thoughtful card, letter of encouragement, or kind Facebook message. At other times, they may take the form of a caring phone call, meaningful visit, or generous check sent in the mail. On other occasions they may look like a kind deed or simple act of service. By reaching out with compassion, you will be making a positive difference in someone else's life while reaping an emotional reward yourself. May the Prince of Peace fill your mind, heart, body, and soul with the joy of the Lord, which is your strength (Neh. 8:10).

§

Blue Task
#5

- Think of three to five tangible yet doable ways to reach out to someone who is "drowning" to bless them by providing your personal support and care. These realistic caregiving ideas each represent a powerful lifeline.
- Choose one of the ideas you've thought of and follow through with it in the next forty-eight to seventy-two hours, if at all possible.
- Gradually develop a longer list of potential lifeline service opportunities. This way, you will have several good, practical thoughts on the ready for when the opportunity arises for you to mobilize into service mode.

Chapter Six

Until You Walk a Mile in My Shoes

TOO often, those who suffer with depression don't receive the kind of consistent, compassionate, nonjudgmental support they desperately need from their loved ones. I wish I could say that I'd always been supportive and understanding, but unfortunately that's simply not the case. At times I grew impatient and frustrated, even angry with Missy for being unable to snap out of it and meet her responsibilities. I haven't always been kind and considerate toward her ongoing, chronic condition. My own selfishness and unfair expectations caused me to act in inexcusable and embarrassingly harsh ways.

§

If you've been on the receiving end of unkind criticism for your depression, you know firsthand just how painful that can be. Unfortunately, melancholia is often mistaken for self-pity, negativity, defeatism, or laziness. People who don't struggle with these issues have difficulty understanding what it's like for the sufferer. Those who go through it are made to feel less-than and ashamed of their malady.

How can you be mindful of others who have been unfairly criticized and misunderstood? Among this group are recovering addicts, divorcees, single parents, unemployed or underemployed persons, those on welfare, and victims of abuse and/or domestic violence. There are also those persons that suffer with chronic medical conditions resulting in a perpetual state of tiredness or sluggishness such as myalgic encephalomyelitis/chronic fatigue syndrome (ME/CFS), fibromyalgia, hypothyroidism, or hyperthyroidism. Furthermore, there are those with learning, physical, or emotional disabilities. Heighten your awareness of others and be looking for someone to reach out to who is drowning emotionally. Increase your internal radar's sensitivity to those around you that are struggling to stay afloat. Give a word of encouragement to them. Look for someone who appears exhausted, downcast, and may need a real friend.

Maybe you're unsure about being labeled as "depressed" because it doesn't fit into your mental image of victorious living. Until the last couple of decades, depression carried a greater stigma within the church than it does now. People who suffered with this invisible medical disorder were sometimes viewed as weak, self-pitying, and faithless. Misguided individuals would think, if not actually say out loud, "If only _____ possessed more faith, she could get over her depression." Ironically, it is often their faith in God that helps them hold on. Knowing that God sees you and loves you as you are can help make the bad days tolerable and give you hope that a good day will come again.

Since many non-sufferers minimize the insidiousness of depression, they can't understand the overwhelming effect it may have on someone else's life. Also, because they don't understand its underlying causes, they tend to eschew and criticize those who suffer with it. When Christians take their own lives as a result of deep depression, a lot of people don't know what to make of their tragic action or how to respond to the family in an appropriate way. In August of 2014, when the talented comic Robin Williams passed away, there was a range of helpful and hurtful social media posts from people in the church. My Missy responded to the hurtful comments as follows: "We would not consider having cancer and dying from it unforgiveable, but somehow many believe having depression and dying from it is unforgiveable. Depression is a disease, not a sin. Those struggling with depression are not far from God, but they depend on Him to make it through every day. Until a cure is found for depression and other mental illnesses, the church must move with compassion, not judgment." I could not have said it better myself.

§

Within Christian circles, many have wondered how such an agonizing emotional disorder could be conceivable for faithful believers. For some believers, this challenges their narrow, legalistic theology based on mutually exclusive extremes—on the one hand is depression and on the other is victorious living—the two shall never meet in their black-and-white worldview.

Popular health-and-wealth theologies teach that if you truly believe in God's power to protect and provide, you will be insulated from hardships. Therefore, they reject the basic notion that a faithful Christian can suffer with depression. It doesn't fit into that perspective. Misguided doctrine fosters the false belief that if people simply set their minds on being grateful for their blessings, they will never struggle with depression. Sometimes the use of Scripture can feel oppressive to depressed persons—as if it is being used as a weapon against them. Well-meaning persons who lack personal experience or understanding of depression may resort to "throwing scriptures" at the problem. To the depressed person, it can feel like adding insult to injury, like being sucker punched in the name of Jesus. That's truly unfortunate. God's Word is an invaluable resource that ought to be used to help and comfort, not hurt or blame.

It offends me when I see T-shirts or bumper stickers that promote Pollyanna concepts like the following: "Too blessed to be depressed." This simplistic notion might sound pious, but it perpetuates the fallacy that depression is a decision the sufferer makes. It says that if we just take the time to count our blessings, depression will miraculously disappear, but how would the deaf community feel if a billboard slogan stated: "Too holy to be hearing impaired"? Or, the blind community with an axiom like "Too virtuous to be vision impaired"? Or, what if someone with diabetes saw a sign that said, "Too devout to be diabetic"? Or, a cancer patient: "Too consecrated to have cancer"? They would rightfully be outraged, as would the rest of us. In the same way, depression is real like cancer is real and cannot be dealt with by naïve notions.

Depression can strike regardless of an individual's religious beliefs or degree of spiritual maturity. Just because you're a believer doesn't automatically entitle you to immunity. The refusal to acknowledge depression and handle it appropriately can produce additional problems for those who suffer with it as well as for their families and friends. The sad result is that many good Christian people suffer in silence because they don't feel safe opening up to anyone about their problems for fear of being judged. Holding it in, however, is unhealthy. In fact, untreated desolation will eventually cause those with depression to implode, which can lead to irreparable psychological and spiritual damage.

§

There's far more to someone than just depression. Sometimes, that's an easy point to miss. Our identity and value far exceed any one facet of our lives, either good or bad. Like many, I used to hold certain biases that caused me to underestimate depression's power in people's lives. Quite frankly, in my younger years I was a bit holier-than-thou, naïve, and uninformed. I'm grateful for those who challenged my thinking and deepened my understanding. So, before you judge yourself or your loved one too harshly, remind yourself that depression is a real disease. Just like other illnesses, you will have good days and bad days. Feeling sequestered and unable to share your heavy burden with supportive friends and family ultimately becomes simply too much to bear, so do what you can on the good days, and give yourself or your loved one some compassion on the bad days.

§

Blue Task #6

- Go to my website, RyanNoelFraser.com, and watch the short video called *There's much more to you than depression*.
- After watching the video, write down a list of ten things besides depression that positively define you and make you who you are.
- Think of someone you know who could likely use a word of encouragement. Write them a thoughtful letter or send them a "Thinking of you" card just to show them you care about them and are praying for them.

Chapter Seven

Shades of Blue

Blue *used to* be my favorite color. As a child, I was captivated by how the majestic, azure blue tints of the South African summer sky sank behind the sparkling cobalt and navy-blue horizon of the vast Atlantic Ocean. In those earliest, carefree days, to me blue represented all that was natural, carefree, and happy. It reminded me of pure freedom and joy. Blue was beautiful.

Did you know that the Crayola color wheel has nineteen different shades of blue? Since the company's inception in 1903, Crayola has devised more and more shades of blue. In fact, the nineteen different variations represented in their standard crayon box only touches the hem of the garment with roughly fifty-five or fifty-six shades of blue. The blue color spectrum is rather impressive.

As a little boy, I quickly came to associate the color blue with masculinity and strength. In reminded me of the handsome uniforms worn by military personnel who served in the South African Navy and Air Force. To me, blue represented greatness, glory, and grandeur. In my youthful innocence, I never entertained the remote possibility of *blueness* ever representing something else, something far more negative in nature, sinister, and ominous.

§

What's Your Present Shade?

Depression or melancholia comes in many different forms, or *shades of blue,* if you will. It is definitely not a monochromatic disease with uniform symptoms. Depression manifests itself differently for different people. That is why it's so important to avoid stereotyping yourself or others who may be struggling with depression in their lives. Each person's symptoms and presence or degree of the various types of depression is unique. One size certainly doesn't fit all.

When Missy had different levels of depression and I was unable to relate to her suffering, we decided to classify her feelings by various shades of color, mostly in the blue spectrum. Here are the four levels we came up with. Please remember when you read through these levels that they're not linear. The levels of depression are dynamic and fluid and, therefore, you can move from any level of intensity to another level. Keep in mind, level four is not the end; you will transition to another level again.

- **Level One: Sunshine Yellow**

A day that is sunshine yellow is an easy day to be alive. You feel like you can keep up with your daily tasks and still have room to smile. You may even take on a creative task. You are grateful to God to see things more clearly today. The fog has cleared. You, therefore, try to get as much done as you possibly can on these days, because you know the nature of your disease and know the bad days will return. However, for the time being, you count your blessings and wish this day would never come to an end.

- **Level Two: Sky Blue**

A day that is sky blue is a manageable day. You can feel the shadow of depression around you, but you can still see the sunshine peeking through the clouds. You soldier on and are grateful that you can still function as needed for your family and friends and take care of your daily responsibilities.

Level Three: Violet Blue

A day that is violet blue is a hard day. It reminds you that everything is getting darker again. You have trouble doing what needs to be done for yourself and others. You feel the weight of the shadow of depression enveloping you. You are sad, but don't know why. Sometimes it is hard to move or even breathe. Your body aches and you miss the sunshine days. You struggle to get the day's tasks done.

Level Four: Dark Indigo

A day that is dark indigo is difficult to talk about. You struggle to move at all. You find everything challenging. Getting up, dressing, brushing your teeth, and putting one foot in front of the other seem like insurmountable hurdles—impossible tasks. Everything hurts: your body, your mind, and your relationships. You feel very little hope of seeing a sunshine day again. You are overwhelmed with sadness and you even wonder if anyone cares at all. These are the days you wish to be with God and ease the burden you think you are to your family. This is the darkest shade of blue before everything goes black.

§

Forms of Depression

There are multiple categories among the various recognizable types of depression. Sometimes it is challenging to diagnose the disorder, especially when there are other variables and non-depression related symptoms present in the mix. Clinicians must then develop a differential (or comorbid) diagnosis, which takes these other symptoms and problems into appropriate consideration.

The recognized forms of depression include:

1. **Dysthymia:** what I view as a milder form of depression;
2. **Major depressive disorder:** this represents a long-term malady;
3. **Post-partum depression**: this comes with a variety of symptoms depending on the particular woman during the months following giving birth to a child;
4. **Grief-related depression:** when one experiences the death of a loved one or family member, or experiences a disappointment or broken relationship;
5. **Guilt or shame-related depression**: can be linked either to appropriate guilt/shame based on personal moral failures or to false (or neurotic) guilt/shame stemming from victimization such as childhood abuse;
6. **Situational or trauma-related depression**, triggered by difficult life circumstances such as various crises or traumas which result in people feeling overwhelmed, anxiety-ridden, and losing hope;
7. **Physiologically and/or neurochemically related depression**: may result from the physical/biological trauma of major surgeries and/or side-effects of pre-scribed medication;
8. **Bipolar I & II**: also sometimes referred to as manic depression;
9. **Seasonal affective disorder**: also known by the acronym SAD; and
10. **Anfechtungen:** suffering related to spiritual depression; sometimes referred to as "The Dark Night of the Soul," based off the poem by the sixteenth century Spanish mystic and poet, St. John of the Cross. In fact, the great reformer, Martin Luther, confessed to suffering at times in his life with this last form of depression.

§

The Big Seven

In working with depressed clients, I've developed what I refer to as "the big seven" areas for them to consider. In yours or a loved one's battle with depression, it is important to take a holistic and well-balanced approach to alleviating the suffering. The respective seven essential areas that need to be attended to include the following:

1. Medical/medicinal
2. Regular physical exercise
3. Well-balanced dietary plan
4. Recreational strategy (i.e., things they do to take a break/rest/relax)
5. Meaningful spirituality (particularly their practice of spiritual disciplines such as prayer, Scripture reading, meditation, etc., and spiritual service to others)
6. Healthy relationships (to self, others, and God)
7. Existential concerns (such as making sense of personal suffering, identity in Christ, and life purpose)

In particular, out of the above seven important areas, when the medical/medicinal, relational, and spiritual components are imbalanced, the inevitable result will be cognitive distortions or faulty logic and inaccurate perceptions. That is precisely why it is so important to take a balanced approach to treating depression symptoms and their underlying causes.

Yes, depression comes in many levels (or shades of blue). What level are you today? And how are you strategically responding to it?

§

Blue Task
#7

- Go to my website, RyanNoelFraser.com, and watch the short video called *The Many Shades of Blue* located on the "Blues Video Resources" page.
- On four 3x5 notecards:

  1. Label your first notecard "Sunshine Yellow" (Please feel free to color it in if you like);
  2. Label your second notecard "Sky Blue";
  3. Label your third notecard "Violet Blue";
  4. Label your fourth notecard "Dark Indigo."

After all your notecards are labeled, turn each of them over and write the symptoms you experience on those particular days.

Next, find a trustworthy friend (or group of friends) with whom you feel safe discussing your particular shade of blue and how you are trying to live victoriously despite your struggle.

Depending on your current shade of blue, think through how you need to respond and what proactive steps to take so far as they relate to personal care and outreach to others.

Chapter Eight

Knocked Down,
But Not Defeated

Do you ever feel like a boxer in the ring, knocked down and unable to get your legs back underneath you to stand up? The apostle Paul often felt beaten down, but he never gave up. He puts it this way in 2 Corinthians 4:8-9 (NIV): "We are hard pressed on every side, but not crushed; perplexed, but not in despair; persecuted, but not abandoned; struck down, but not destroyed." Depression may have you on the ropes or knocked down on the mat, but you're not defeated. Keep on getting back up. Keep on fighting for your life. However, if you're going to successfully fight against depression, you need to know the opposing forces you're up against.

§

A simple analogy here might be helpful. You can compare a depressed person's brain to a circuit board, one in which several of the "on/off" switches aren't working properly. The whole electrical system is thrown into disarray. How can someone be held responsible for a problem that is largely beyond their own control? It doesn't matter how spiritually minded or religiously faithful someone is; depression is no respecter of persons, and impacts individuals at all levels of spiritual maturity. No one is exempt. To get down on oneself for feeling depressed, or to criticize those who struggle with it, is blaming victims for a disease over which they have little to no control. It's unkind and unfair. So, please be kind to yourself and patient with others.

§

Symptoms of the Dreaded "D" Word

There are several common symptoms of depression. Though every sufferer's experience of it is unique, potential indicators include the following:

- Having trouble concentrating, making decisions, remembering details
- Relentlessly feeling fatigued and experiencing a noticeable decrease in energy
- Struggling with feelings of guilt, worthlessness, and/or helplessness
- Facing unshakeable feelings of hopelessness or pessimism
- Experiencing insomnia, including waking up too early
- Sleeping too much
- Displaying irritability or a sense of restlessness
- Experiencing a loss of interest in various activities or hobbies you once enjoyed
- Lacking sexual desire or overactive sexual desire
- Overeating or undergoing a loss of appetite
- Experiencing persistent aches and pains, headaches, cramps, or digestive problems that don't respond to treatment
- Being plagued by perpetual sadness, anxiety, or feelings of emptiness
- Fantasizing about or making plans to kill yourself
- Attempting to commit suicide

These are serious symptoms that deserve your attention and warrant further exploration and proactive treatment with qualified mental health and/or medical professionals.

§

Problematic Patterns

Depression, at times, places annoying obstacles in my path, crushes my creativity, and impedes my progress. It robs me of my sense of purpose and inhibits my ability to function effectively. I despise depression because it makes me grouchy, quick-tempered, pessimistic, lethargic, and apathetic. Moreover, depression predisposes me to self-absorption and self-loathing. No, I'm not a big fan! And, let me venture to guess, you're reading this book because you're not a fan, either.

As I reflect upon my life, I recognize a consistent pattern of highs and lows that occur in a cyclical fashion. The emotional cycle is predictable in some ways, but unpredictable in others. Why these constant ups and downs, peaks and valleys? It's probable that a number of causes have contributed in both perceptible and imperceptible ways. Likely influencers have included significant losses, health concerns, spiritual mindset, job demands, dietary patterns, exercise regimen, relational conflicts, financial stress, and more. Sometimes it's easier to pinpoint one or two primary triggers, while on other occasions the direct cause is less obvious.

§

Psychological Pain and Hopelessness

As a clinical pastoral therapist and minister, I've spent a considerable amount of time with depressed clients, good people who often suffer in silence. Their pain is profound—almost palpable. Depression, like a cruel and merciless mercenary, has grabbed them in a chokehold. The enemy has been slowly but surely strangling the spiritual and emotional life out of them. The sparkle is noticeably absent from their eyes. Their body language and non-verbals tell the tale. In exasperation they ask, "What's wrong with me? Why do I feel so down all the time? Why can't I seem to shake this darkness?" For some, tears come quickly; for others, they appear to be all cried out. Hope hangs in the balance.

Depression manifests itself in diverse ways in people's lives, creating a broad spectrum of problems and difficulties. But before I go further, I want to emphasize one important thing: The presence of depression in someone's life isn't indicative of God's judgment or disapproval. Romans 8:1 (ESV) states, "There is . . . now no condemnation for those who are in Christ Jesus."

As your loving and compassionate parent, God cares deeply about you in your depression and hurts for you in the midst of your distress. Never forget that.

§

Depression's dark presence first infiltrates the recesses of your mind, permeates your personality, and then makes its way into all corners of your existence, ransacking your emotional house. Perhaps you've already tried therapy, read self-help books, taken prescribed psychotropic medication (antidepressants), or self-medicated. You're frustrated, and understandably so. Depression ambushes your emotions, drains your physical energy, intrudes upon your spirituality, keeps you awake at night or makes you sleep too much, and generally encumbers your life. Simple tasks like getting out of bed in the morning, taking care of personal hygiene, grooming and getting dressed for the day, or preparing breakfast can become huge challenges. Depression can also negatively impact your ability to invest in personal relationships at home, school, work, church, and in the community.

Your marriage suffers. Friendships flail. You're impaired in your everyday interactions with others.

Melancholy can rob you of the spiritual joy and abundant life that Jesus came to offer believers. Inner peace is vandalized. Hope is hit hard. Proverbs 17:22 (ESV) declares, "A joyful heart is good medicine, but a crushed spirit dries up the bones." Your personal sense of well-being and determination disintegrate into dust. You may feel that if only you possessed enough faith you wouldn't have those emotional struggles. The shame can be unbearable at times. Your spirituality suffers. Internal turmoil triggers your downward spiral, which is fed by confusion, false guilt, and hopelessness. Oftentimes, a flawed idea invades your thoughts that "God is mad at me for some reason and is punishing me." Or, "I must deserve this and am paying penance for my sins." Indeed, distortion in cognitive processing is a well-known symptom of depression itself. If you personify depression as an intruder or unwelcome visitor, how does it look, sound, and behave? What types of things does it say and do to intimidate you and keep you in a weakened state? And what does melancholia con you into believing about yourself and your future?

You don't have to see depression as a symptom of faithlessness or a guilty conscience. Rather, it's a debilitating medical disorder, caused by a neurochemical imbalance that may be passed down genetically, and it ought to be treated as such. I've counseled godly leaders who were thinking about resigning their ministries due to their painful battle with depression. Their self-esteem and confidence had been all but destroyed. But, in my view, there are positive aspects of depression. For example, those same church leaders possess tremendous insight, wisdom, and empathy because of their personal experience with depression. With their unparalleled capacity for genuine concern, they are a valuable resource to others.

If you're a clergy person or lay leader in church and are suffering with depression, please don't quit. Seek appropriate help to get you over the hump. You're critically important to God's kingdom, and your personal perspective and hard-earned wisdom are desperately needed. Your personal experience and voice count.

§

There are numerous biblical examples of people of great faith who seemed to struggle with depression. Certain well-known biblical characters all had identifiable struggles.

- **Shiphrah and Puah**, the two Hebrew midwives, were faced with the burden of fighting the genocide of Hebrew baby boys in Egypt (Exod. 1:8–2:10).
- **Moses** dealt with the constant grumbling and complaining of the people of Israel (Exod. 16) and was overworked (Exod. 18:13-18).
- **David** bore the unbearable guilt of his sin with Bathsheba (2 Sam. 11-12) and the disloyalty and death of his son (2 Sam. 18:19-33).
- **Balaam** was sulky and depressed when he did not get what he wanted (Num. 22:20-21).
- **Elijah** felt he was the last faithful follower of God, ran for his life, and was physically and emotionally exhausted (1 Kings 19:1-18).
- **Hannah**, unable to bear children, was criticized by her rival, and felt like a complete failure as a wife (1 Sam. 1:1-16).
- **Paul** was falsely accused of being in the ministry for selfish reasons (2 Cor. 10:1-12), and he faced severe physical and emotional suffering and abuse (2 Cor. 11:16-29).

The priestly sons of Korah wrote psalms that hint at depressive symptoms. For example, the author of Psalm 42:3-5 acknowledges his melancholic condition. He's troubled by it but not completely dismayed or dejected. The writer remains committed to trust in his Creator for deliverance.

In the midst of his distress and downcast feelings, this sufferer reveals his faith as he states, "Deep calls to deep at the roar of your waterfalls; all your breakers and your waves have gone over me. By day the LORD commands his steadfast love, and at night his song is with me, a prayer to the God of my life" (vs. 7-8). While confessing his disquieting emotions, he is able to remain faithful to God and acknowledge God's preservation and presence in his life. He is knocked down, but not defeated. The writer is tenaciously holding onto hope. You might feel a bit hopeless right now and wonder if your condition will ever improve, but God is always with you, even in your darkest hours. Whatever you do, please don't give up.

§

I used to believe that God never gives us more than we can handle by ourselves. Like many Christians, I had internalized that flawed theological idea from an erroneous application of 1 Corinthians 10:13. The verse actually promises that God won't allow the devil to tempt us beyond the limits of what we are able to withstand, and he will always provide us with a way of escape—an avenue to resist the temptation. It's often misunderstood and misappropriated. It eased my mind to believe that God would never let me endure trials or tribulations beyond my ability to cope with them. However, the promise is protection against temptations, not insulation from trials.

I now believe God can allow us to be forced to our knees to fully depend on him. I came to this conclusion when my four-year-old son was diagnosed with a life-threatening illness. My world imploded because that was a crisis that was more than I could bear. My spirit was crushed under the unbearable burden of despair I felt and it drove me to my knees as I cried out to God. The ordeal of my son's illness taught me many valuable lessons. One was that sometimes we feel tested beyond our human capacity to endure, so that we're forced to relinquish our illusion of control and trust Him to handle things. That life lesson transformed us and shaped us in the refiner's fire. We also had to learn to totally surrender to our gracious and loving God. God sustained our family through extreme duress and gut-wrenching emotional pain. Thankfully our son was cured of cancer. We now recognize that we couldn't have survived the adversity on our own. It was beyond our capacity to bear alone.

I've since learned that depression can push you to beyond the threshold of your psycho-spiritual limits. Our human frailty is laid bare. An inordinate amount of faith and courage is needed to survive depression's vicious onslaught, forcing us to dig deeper. The lesson is learning to develop greater faith and reliance on God in light of our struggle. Nowadays, I tend to lean more on the sentiment of Philippians 4:13 that states, "I can do all things through him who strengthens me" (ESV), because I've come to realize that I most certainly cannot handle life's struggles by myself. I need God's help and strength daily to see me through. And nothing is impossible with God (Luke 1:37).

§

Depression is only one facet of your life. It doesn't need to hinder your walk with God, but it can push you into a deeper walk. The devil desires to make you a victim, and God doesn't want you to live in the victim mentality. He intends for you to live victoriously. Romans 8:37-39 (NIV) states: "No, in all these things we are *more than conquerors* [emphasis mine] through him who loved us. For I am convinced that neither death nor life, neither angels nor demons, neither the present nor the future, nor any powers, neither height nor depth, nor anything else in all creation, will be able to separate us from the love of God that is in Christ Jesus our Lord." To be *more than a conqueror* implies winning in the end. The source of your strength is his unfailing love in your life.

Scripture assures you that faith is the victory that overcomes the world (1 John 5:4). Possessing spiritual fortitude doesn't mean you'll never be afraid. Quite the opposite. It simply means continuing to hope in God despite your fears, anxieties, and the seemingly insurmountable obstacles before you. Courage is facing your fears. Faith means believing that God will see you through because he always fulfills his promises to his children. Courage means never losing heart or giving up the good fight of faith. It means bravely confronting this enemy called depression, while remembering God is ultimately in control. This may be difficult for you, but nothing is impossible with God (Mark 10:27). You're up against not only an external adversary in Satan but also an internal enemy in yourself.

§

It's not uncommon for depressed Christians to have the following kinds of disquieting thoughts in their heads, though they seldom say them out loud:

- "My faith is under attack. I find it hard to pray and almost impossible to force myself to go to church. Why can't I snap out of this depression and be the faithful Christian I desire to be?"
- "Where is God in the midst of my struggle with depression? He doesn't seem to hear my prayers. Does he care about what I'm going through?"
- "Right now, it doesn't feel like God loves me very much. He seems so distant and I feel disconnected from him."
- "In the past, I used to be bold in my faith, but I don't know anymore. My spiritual strength has all but evaporated and I feel discouraged most of the time. My faith is slipping away and I'm really scared."

§

Do you relate to any of the sentiments above? Do you feel your faith in God is being undermined by depression? If so, I remind you once again, melancholia is a *not* a symptom of faithlessness. The apostle Peter writes, "Beloved, do not be surprised at the fiery trial when it comes upon you to test you, as though something strange were happening to you" (1 Pet. 4:12, ESV). Later, he continues: "Be sober-minded; be watchful. Your adversary the devil prowls around like a roaring lion, seeking someone to devour . . . And after you have suffered a little while, the God of all grace, who has called you to his eternal glory in Christ, will himself restore, confirm, strengthen, and establish you" (1 Pet. 5:8-10, ESV). The devil is out to get you. He is a ferocious opponent and seeks any means possible—including the insidious avenue of depression—to destroy your faith and rip your emotional life to pieces. Not even the most faithful believers are spared the misery of his vicious attacks. Just like in the remarkable story of Job, the devil is out to prove to God that your faithful obedience is contingent on his kind generosity and protection from trouble in your life. Satan, the great accuser of Christians (Rev. 12:10), seeks to assassinate your integrity by insinuating that the moment God's protective shield is lowered, and you experience pain, you'll cease loving and serving him. Your challenge is to prove the devil wrong, exposing him to be the liar he is.

There is a spiritual war raging, a fierce power struggle for the allegiance of your soul. Light and darkness are in hand-to-hand combat. Ephesians 6:10-20 describes the epic proportions of this eternal battle. That's why you're instructed to "put on the whole armor of God" to protect yourself and fight against "the spiritual forces of evil in the heavenly places." However, sometimes you may feel like your name is at the top of Satan's hit list. You may ask, "Why me? Why have I been selected to suffer in this way? Will this ever come to an end?" God has the prerogative to place his divine hand of healing upon someone and vanquish depression altogether from a person's life. What if that's not part of his plan for your life? What if, as in the apostle Paul's case, God doesn't remove your struggle but instead says, "My grace is sufficient for you, for my strength is made perfect in weakness" (2 Cor. 12:9)? God can teach you to live with your depression faithfully and courageously. It's possible to bring glory to him in your life despite your struggle with melancholia. God may be calling you to accept your situation and glorify him by setting a positive example by your faithfulness and Christ-like attitude.

No matter who you are as a Christian, you're all fragile, fractured, and flawed, but God has chosen to use you nonetheless to carry the message of his amazing grace within your finite being. You're commissioned to share the good news of peace and salvation with the world. Your particular struggle is depression. Like someone born deaf, blind, or with a heart defect, you have to learn healthy ways of living within your physical and psychological limitations. Once you accept *what is*, you can answer *what's next*. After answering that question you'll be ready to learn many valuable lessons through your difficulties with depression that can't be learned any other way.

Rather than demonizing depression as inherently evil and sinful (or punishment for sin in your life) or dividing depression and faith as mutually exclusive, you can learn to cope faithfully with your condition. That's not easy, but it doesn't have to be a black-and-white quagmire comprised of an all-or-nothing between faithfulness and faithlessness. There is much more gray area to be explored.

There will be times that you don't feel God's presence, but that doesn't mean he's not there sustaining you. God is calling you to faithfulness, whether your day is sunshine yellow, sky blue, violet blue, or dark indigo. And he is actively working in obvious and hidden ways to provide you with the resources to survive your depression. Some days all you will have is your faith. Hold it tight; good days will return. However, while you're in the midst of depression's storm, hope may seem elusive. Remind yourself that the dark indigo days will pass. Remember depression is fluid and you will return to better days. Even though you cannot see hope, hope remains. As a believer, you can rest assured that nothing—not even depression—will ever be able to separate you from God's love. You may feel estranged but that doesn't make it so. No matter your circumstances, and irrespective of where you are emotionally, Jesus won't desert you. He's promised (Hebrews 13:5).

In Acts 27, Paul is sailing on a ship headed for Italy when a gale-force wind strikes. After being violently tossed on the sea for days and jettisoning the cargo and tackle overboard, the vessel strikes a reef and is shipwrecked. With the stern being smashed to pieces by the surf, the passengers who can swim attempt to make for the land. The rest are instructed to grab planks or pieces of the ship and hold on. Eventually all 276 persons are brought safely to the shore.

Right now, hanging on may be best. But you can also reach out for help.

- Ask your minister if you can set up a time to talk.
- Make an appointment with a physician or mental health counselor.
- Seek support from a trusted friend.

Do whatever you can to keep your head above water until help arrives. Your task right now is to survive the storm and not drown.

§

A Melancholic Parent's Burden

If you're a parent—especially of younger children—and suffer with depression, the burden you bear sometimes feels overwhelming. Your task as a caregiver is indeed monumental. And you're likely your own worst critic. You focus on your shortfalls and seemingly miserable failures rather than on your strengths and victories. But lest you have forgotten, let me remind you of something critically important right now: Nobody loves your children more than you do! And nobody loves you more than they do! There's a reason God chose you out of all the people in the world to be their parent. He knew that you were the perfectly imperfect match for your precious children. (Yes, you heard me correctly!) There's no such thing as a perfect parent. We're all flawed at best.

If it's all you can do to take care of yourself, let alone see after your children's needs as well, I'm guessing you struggle with immense guilt and shame. You feel like your kids are being cheated or short-changed because of your illness. You so badly wish you were able to give them more of yourself—a better, healthier version—instead of coming home from work to lie in bed or on the couch and watch TV with them. You would love to be able to do more for them and with them. If you could, you'd attend all their extracurricular activities. You would certainly help to prepare all healthy, home-cooked meals regularly—but you simply can't do it. You would regularly play catch or kick a ball with them. However, the emotional and physical energy is just not there. You wish it was. The guilt inside you is oppressive. It cuts you to the core of your being as a parent. If only you didn't suffer with depression! But truth be told, you're doing the best you can. And nobody can or should expect you to do any more than that. And just for the record, no parent gets it right all the time.

God knows what you're thinking and what you're going through. He certainly understands your unique and difficult situation, and cares about you very much. You see, he is your loving parent! Please don't get the mistaken idea that God is angry or upset with you. Satan loves nothing more than to prey on the sensitive hearts and minds of parents. He wants to destroy your self-esteem and annihilate your will to keep on moving forward in your life—your instinctive desire to keep on molding and nurturing your children. Yes, the devil knows how to hit you where it hurts worst. Nothing can hurt a mother or father more than this! But know without a shadow of a doubt that God is fully aware of how much and how deeply you love your children. Your children can also sense it. You have their best interests at heart. Don't beat yourself up! Please cut yourself some slack! Even on your worst day, you're doing a lot of good for your children simply by being with them. Your consistent presence is worth a whole lot. You can't put a price tag on it.

§

Blue Task #8

- Conduct a personal Bible study by yourself or with a few friends on a specific depressed character that you relate to in the Scriptures.
- Journal on the following guided questions:

  1. What specifically is it about this particular biblical character that you relate to?
  2. How did this biblical character faithfully cope with his/her depression?
  3. How could I implement some of those strategies into my own life?

- If you're a parent or uncle or aunt, think of a small gesture of love you can show to your children, nephews, or nieces. It doesn't have to be anything big—just something thoughtful. It might be an inexpensive gift such as a gift card or tickets to the movies.

Chapter Nine

Keeping It Simple: When Love Reaches Out

"RYAN, I—I—" my wife's convulsive crying prevented her from saying anything more.

"What's going on?"

"Austin . . . leukemia." Missy said more but those were the two words that sunk in.

"Dr. Parkey thinks Austin has leukemia. Please come home right away!"

That morning we'd taken our four-year-old to get his blood tested because of mysterious bruising.

"I'll be there are soon as I can."

After we hung up, my thoughts raced and my chest pounded. By the time I approached the railroad track crossing, I found it difficult to catch my breath and was hyperventilating. Five minutes later I pulled in our driveway, slammed the truck in park, and ran inside. Missy lay in the fetal position on the den's recliner, sobbing.

Just then, the home phone rang. Our family doctor was on the line. The tone of his voice was solemn.

"You need to get Austin to the Cook Children's ER as soon as possible. His white blood count is out of control. The only thing that could logically explain this is leukemia!"

I didn't want to alarm the children. Just then, little Austin ambled into the living room. He had a puzzled look on his chubby little face.

"Why is Mommy crying?"

"Mommy's just a little sad right now but she'll be okay. But we need to take you the hospital because you're sick."

"Am I going to die?"

"You're going to be just fine." A lump formed in my throat. "I'll tell you about it on the way there. Okay?"

He nodded.

I tried to remain composed and snapped orders to the family. Missy managed to pull herself together and started packing. We crammed clothes in suitcases, tossed them in the van, and peeled out of the driveway.

En route to Cook Children's in Fort Worth, I called one of my friends, Duane. Without hesitation he replied, "I'll be waiting on you at the ER when you get there."

On arriving an hour later, we were relieved to see him.

"Tell me what you guys need. How can I be most helpful?"

I struggled to hold it together. He calmed me down.

"I'm sure some members from my church will be arriving soon. I'm not ready to talk to anyone. Please be our liaison."

"Consider it done! I'll stay as long as you need me!" he said.

We huddled together for a brief prayer, needing Duane's help on so many levels. I'll never forget his extraordinary pastoral care on that dreadful day.

§

During the next grueling seven weeks we stayed at the Ronald McDonald House, with one or both of us constantly by Austin's side. Olivia, our sweet daughter who was only seven years old at the time, was there, too. Those first days, it felt as if we were caught in some hellish nightmare from which we couldn't wake up. Each hour seemed to bring more medical personnel in strange garb using space-type technology machines, invasive medical tests, unfamiliar medical terms, injections, brutal spinal taps, and toxic chemo infusions for our precious son. What had seemed so important to us pre-diagnosis didn't matter now. Though we never felt abandoned by God, we desperately needed the hands-on support of our church family and friends to survive this ordeal.

Besides the internal anguish we experienced on being informed of our son's cancer, the next most painful blow was the massive disappointment that several persons, whom we had thought were friends we could count on, never came to visit. It's possible that they felt ill-equipped to help and simply didn't want to intrude or get in the way. However, certain individuals made personal sacrifices to be there for us. Some traveled great distances just to hold our hands, offer an empathetic ear, pray over us, and help make the long days a bit more tolerable. Most weren't trained ministers or counselors, but just wonderful individuals who cared. Sometimes the conversation became stilted or awkward, and on occasion there was more silence than talking, but that didn't matter nearly as much as just having them there, willing to listen, offering a shoulder to cry on, and often crying right along with us. Although many came, I especially want to mention one individual named B. J. Lowery.

§

We were surprised when B. J. timidly poked his head through the door of Austin's hospital room. He wore a white cowboy hat, plaid shirt, blue jeans, and brown work boots.

"Hi, guys. How are you making it?" he said with a friendly smile and a Texan drawl. "I love you and Austin and just wanted to be here. Do you mind if I sit with you a while?"

"Sure, B. J. Please come on in!"

Of course, we were happy to have B. J.'s company. We loved and appreciated him. In the past, he had always made an extra effort to show special kindness to our children and us.

B. J. sat unassumingly in Austin's low-lit, cramped hospital room with us, not taking the chair beside his bed, but the one next to the wall. While other visitors came and went, and medical staff went about their perfunctory tasks, B. J. sat quietly, rarely saying anything.

When the announcement over the loudspeaker echoed through the hallways, signifying the end of visiting hours. B. J. stood up to leave and grabbed his hat.

"I love you, Austin. We'll go fishing together when you get back home."

"I love you, too."

We knew B. J. meant it. He didn't say much, but his comforting presence meant a lot to us.

Austin did get to go fishing with B. J. a few months later on his ranch.

The next three years our lives revolved around weekly chemotherapy treatments at Cook Children's and then St. Jude Children's Research Hospital in Memphis. Our son survived and is in full remission.

§

I learned many valuable lessons about caregiving from those who came to our family's aid during Austin's life-threatening illness and treatments.

Here are some of the poignant things I grasped.

Even if we don't have the right words to say, and if it makes us feel awkward and uncomfortable, just being there is enough. Silence is okay. Presence is most important.

The right thing may be simply to hug the individual, quietly holding them in our arms. In this way we can communicate without a single word. At other times, we may just need to sit beside them, holding their hand or gently putting ours on their shoulder. In some situations, we may need to remain a short distance away in silence, demonstrating genuine empathy and loving concern by our gentle presence.

The key is to show up—in person, to be there for them.

Here are three simple suggestions to care for someone in need:

First, *go to them*. When it is uncomfortable. When it is inconvenient. When we don't feel qualified. When we struggle with fear and self-doubt concerning our lack of abilities and know-how. It's difficult to care as Jesus cared without showing up. Jesus went to where the people were. He never rested passively while expecting people to find him (though they often did). We too must go to them.

Second, *listen to them*. So many hurting people just need to talk to someone, to be able to tell their story to a caring person who will listen without passing judgment. Mindlessly repeating trite axioms or offering unsolicited advice isn't helpful. Many times, we hear people but don't really pay attention to what they are saying. We fail to pick up on the fear or sadness in their voice. We are unaware of the heavy burden they are bearing. We fail to grasp the deeper meaning behind the surface content of their words. Our tendency is to speak rather than listen, to give hasty advice instead of being a sounding board, and to rush to a solution instead of simply letting the person unload.

Third, *serve them*. Figure out ways how you may be of assistance. What can you do to ease their burden? Are there tasks that need to be handled, calls that need making, meals that need preparing, a lawn that needs mowing, dogs that need feeding and walking, sheets that need changing, floors that need sweeping and mopping, children that need watching, shoes that need shining, bills that need paying, cars that need fixing, or laundry that needs washing? Follow through and do whatever needs to be done. People need *hands-on* service. Small acts of kindness can brighten the day of someone who is feeling overwhelmed by life's troubles and ignored or forgotten by others. Never underestimate the power of a thoughtful deed, no matter how insignificant it may appear to be. It can breathe new life into a person's suffocating spirit and revive their careworn soul. Who do you know in your sphere of influence that could use a phone call, visit, and/or act of service?

§

Blue Task
#9

- Think of three people you know, particularly individuals who have chronically ill or special needs children, and intentionally begin praying for them by name this week.
- When praying for those individuals, ask God for the wisdom to know how best you may be able to reach out to them with the love of Christ.
- Make a plan to be physically present, if possible, to serve those individuals and their children.

Chapter Ten

From Despair to Hope and Healing

I turned to Missy and smiled gently. "It's going to be okay, Honey," I whispered, almost as if trying to reassure myself as much as her. We were waiting apprehensively in the nephrologist's office to find out the results from my wife's kidney biopsy. Missy's beautiful, long blonde hair glistened and her cheeks had a soft pinkish hue. From all outward appearances, she was the picture of health for a twenty-year-old woman. But, sadly, she wasn't.

She fidgeted with her fingers and bounced her knee to self-soothe, lost in thought and extremely nervous about what we would shortly find out. It had been a stressful and frustrating four months of a number of unfruitful consultations with various medical specialists. We desperately needed to get definitive answers to Missy's unusual physical symptoms.

I heard the click-clack of footsteps coming down the clinic's tile hallway. "I think he's coming." I sat up in preparation. In walked the nephrologist wearing a white lab coat. He took a seat across from us behind his neatly organized, expensive cherry-wood desk. Behind him were well-appointed bookshelves with various medical works interspersed with tasteful decorations.

The doctor appeared pensive and somber. I felt like he was struggling to maintain eye contact with us.

"I'm afraid I've got some discouraging news from the tests." He sighed and gazed over at Missy. "You have an acute kidney disease. It's called focal sclerosing glomerulonephritis." His words stung, though his East Indian accent possessed a warm and compassionate tone.

The tears Missy had been fighting back now washed over her face. I clasped her right hand with both of mine as we absorbed the upsetting news.

The doctor furrowed his brow as he continued. "Your kidneys don't filter waste products and toxins from your blood properly. Therefore, you have elevated creatinine levels in your blood and protein in your urine. Eventually, you'll have to go on dialysis."

"Could you please repeat that?" I found his medical jargon confusing. "What's the name of the disease again?" I felt it was important for me to remember everything he was saying so I could repeat it back to Missy later as well as to our relatives.

Missy began to tremble, so I scooted my chair closer to hers and put my arm around her. She hunched forward.

"I know this is a lot to take in. I'm sorry to overwhelm you with so much information all at once. I'll write everything down for you," the doctor said. "But we have a lot to talk about."

I nodded silently.

"Does this mean I'm going to have to go on dialysis right away?" Missy asked.

"Not for quite a while. But we can't be sure. Your kidneys are currently functioning at 50 percent."

He informed us that this particular disease was unusual in younger adults and usually only occurred in the geriatric population. That didn't make either of us feel any better. Tears welled up in my eyes.

Though various specialists predicted that Missy's kidneys would likely only last for up to another eight years, her kidneys survived for eighteen. We count it as a blessing. However, by then, they were functioning at 17 percent. We consulted with renal specialists at Vanderbilt Medical Center in Nashville who recommended she be put on a donor list for a transplant before resorting to dialysis. In their opinion, following this proactive strategy would increase the potential for a successful transplant.

I lost much sleep over my wife's critical condition. I tossed and turned in bed at night. My temples throbbed whenever I thought about it. Sometimes, Missy would talk in her sleep as her unconscious mind tried to come to terms with the tremendous emotional stress she was under. My heart ached for her. I wanted to help in whatever way possible, but I struggled to know how best to support Missy and be there for her. I was blessed to be in good health and my blood was O-positive, which could be donated to people of any blood type without fear of rejection. Over several days I prayed about it and weighed out the pros and cons of giving her one of my kidneys. This wasn't the first time the thought had crossed my mind as I had had nearly two decades to think about it. But it still wasn't an easy decision. What would donating one of my kidneys mean to my own health? Was I willing to put my life in jeopardy? And what about the children's future? Who would take care of them if I didn't survive and Missy remained chronically ill? She would lack the necessary energy to carry out her respective parental responsibilities. These types of questions and thoughts plagued me for quite some time, but my deep love for Missy triumphed.

I volunteered to donate one of my kidneys.

We went to Nashville where the kidney transplant team at Vanderbilt put me through an extensive battery of tests. There was blood work, x-rays, MRIs, a heart stress test, plus various psychological interviews. When they informed us, a few days later, that the compatibility analyses revealed I was going to be a suitable match, we were elated. After consulting with the surgeons, we made plans for the transplant. The team of specialists scheduled a surgery date and we started to count down the days.

In the meantime, Missy and I fretted about how we would manage the long recovery without having family nearby. Our closest relatives lived more than two hours away but our young children needed constant care that neither of us would be able to provide during the weeks after surgery. We hoped our blood relatives and church family would come through for us, but we didn't want to presume or ask. It was a lot to expect of them. When we shared the news of our plans with our immediate family and friends and solicited their support, they had mixed reactions of both excitement and concern. The fear of either of us having medical complications during surgery or afterward was a real concern, but simultaneously there was also anticipation of positive outcomes. We hoped Missy would feel much better and gain renewed strength and energy.

§

A couple of weeks before the scheduled surgery, I received a phone call from the transplant coordinator at the hospital. I took it in my comfortable home office. My initial thought was that she just wanted to clarify a few things about the schedule.

"The transplant team reevaluated your MRIs and has discovered some serious problems. It turns out your kidneys are connected in a complicated way to an unusually large number of arteries, veins, and blood vessels," she said.

I sensed from the disappointed tone in her voice what was about to come next, so I prepared for the blow. "Please God, please God," I repeated in my head.

"The surgeons have decided that kidney removal surgery will prove too risky. Your health and life would be in danger and your transplanted kidney would likely not survive the trauma, so they've called off the surgery."

My heart sank and my stomach instantly got all knotted up. I shut my eyes tightly in unspeakable disappointment. I couldn't bear the thought of having to break the devastating news to Missy.

"Mr. Fraser, are you still there?"

I took a deep breath and expelled the air with a loud whoosh. "So, what do we do next?" I asked the transplant coordinator in desperation.

"We can put Missy's name on the kidney donor waiting list."

I shook my head in frustration and disbelief. "And how long will that take?"

"It usually takes a long time to find a suitable donor."

"What do you mean by *long time? Weeks? Months?*"

"I'm sorry but I can't give you an answer for that because there are many variables involved." It sounded to me like she was trying to hold out hope but in a realistic and cautiously optimistic way.

A feeling of helplessness suddenly came over me. I gulped a sudden buildup of saliva, struggling to swallow as my throat tightened. "Is it okay for us to search for potential donors ourselves?"

"That's a good idea. We wholeheartedly encourage it. Otherwise, Missy will likely need to go on dialysis soon."

"Does that mean she's *that* sick?" I already knew the answer to that question, but couldn't keep myself from asking.

It seemed Missy's receiving a transplant was a long shot. Though I didn't like the odds, I wasn't about to accept defeat. "I'll talk things over with Missy and see what she wants to do."

After hanging up, I slowly walked into the living room with my head hanging low where Missy was watching TV. "I've got some disappointing news. The transplant has been called off."

"What happened?" The color drained from Missy's face. She looked panicky and her lips began to quiver. I shook my head.

It felt we'd both been assaulted. To see my wife suffering in this way hurt deeply and made me feel dejected and powerless.

I shared with Missy the basic details of what the transplant coordinator had told me. And the more I spoke, the more despondent Missy looked. I tenderly held her in my arms, while we both wept. The smell of her freshly washed strawberry-scented hair filled my nostrils. At that moment, all I could think about was how I loved her scent and did not want to live without her. Her tears rubbed off on my cheeks.

As the tears poured out of me, my emotions shifted abruptly. Anger began to burn inside of me. I was furious at the situation—at God.

I suddenly needed to be alone to process what had just happened, so I let go of Missy and walked down the hallway to our master bathroom, locking the door behind me. As I sat on the ledge of the tub, I silently cried out, "God, why are you letting this happen to us? This isn't fair!" Daylight filtered through the glass block windows and danced across the tile floor. Off and on through the day and night I prayed fervently for God to intervene. It was nearly impossible to fall asleep. I felt keyed up and restless, though emotionally exhausted. I lay in bed awake listening to Missy's labored breathing as she incoherently muttered to herself and cried in her sleep.

The next morning, I rose up early with renewed focus and energy. I'd been strategizing most of the night on how to proceed. I walked through to my office, sat down at the desk, and composed an urgent plea on my computer to family, friends, and acquaintances, begging for them to either donate a kidney or to spread the word about Missy's urgent need. I sent out the message via social media outlets and my email list to as many people as I could possibly think of. I figured we had absolutely nothing to lose and everything to gain.

§

A couple of days later, I received an unexpected phone call from a dear friend, Steven Yeakley, whom I had been in ministry with in Wichita Falls, Texas before moving to Tennessee. He sounded concerned. "Yesterday at church some ladies were talking in the kitchen, and I overheard them mention Missy's situation. Tell me more."

I explained what had happened, and Steven asked me several pointed questions. I kept wondering if Steven called as a caring friend or if he perhaps knew someone who was thinking about helping us. After a few seconds of silence, he said, "I want to be evaluated to see if I can donate one of my kidneys to Missy."

I was is such a state of shock that I almost missed his next words. "My blood type is B positive just like Missy's."

I sat upright in my chair and looked up to the ceiling—as if to heaven—and silently thanked God. My skin tingled with goose bumps as a wave of elation and joy came over me.

"You do realize there are serious risks involved—right?"

"I've done quite a bit of research, prayed a lot about it, and talked things over with Shelley. And by the way—in case you're wondering—she's 100 percent on board with it. What do we need to do to get the process started?"

I felt an overwhelming sense of gratitude and relief. Hope bubbled up inside of me. I gave Steven all the particulars and the contact information at Vanderbilt. Immediately after hanging up, I hurried into the living room where Missy was watching TV to share the news.

"Steven Yeakley just called and—you'll never guess what—he says he wants to get tested to see if he can donate a kidney to you." I choked up. Missy started to sob. I knelt down beside where Missy was sitting on the couch and offered a prayer of praise and thanksgiving. We hugged each other, laughing and crying all at once, with indescribable joy and relief.

A week later, after Steven made a preliminary thirteen-hour road trip with his mother to Vanderbilt, the evaluation came back: he was a match. The transplant team scheduled the surgery and less than a month later it took place. On the day of the surgery, several friends and family members gathered in the hospital waiting area in anticipation, occasionally circling up to hold hands and pray fervently for both Missy and Steven as well as for the surgical team. The seven-hour surgery was successful. The waiting area erupted with spontaneous applause and celebration when the word came.

While Missy was recovering in the hospital, our son Austin was receiving chemotherapy at St. Jude in Memphis. My brother Stuart took him to his infusion appointment, so I could stay by Missy's side. Stuart's thirteen-year old daughter, Camille, had only just finished chemotherapy treatments herself for bone cancer (osteosarcoma) six months prior at Vanderbilt Children's.

On the outside of the door of Missy's hospital room, I taped up a poster she'd created the day before surgery. It said: "I am weak, but He is strong." I overheard an R.N. at the nearby nurses' station commenting to staff, "Have you read the sign on her door? I think it's so great."

§

During Missy's surgery and lengthy recovery, we were inundated with countless expressions of concern and compassionate deeds from many people. Missy's dad came from Kansas to be by her side. I remember Missy saying before surgery to her father, "It will be okay, Dad. Either way I win. If I make it through surgery, I get to see you and Ryan and the kids again. If I don't make it through surgery, I get to see Mom again." On returning home, my mother stayed with us for several days to help out with the children and household chores. After family was gone, our church family took over.

Our care group from church mobilized to provide meals for an entire month. A kind and generous friend named Lisa prepaid for five house cleanings by a professional housekeeping service. Alice, another sweet lady from church, transported our children to and from school each day. Other individuals gave us cash or gift cards to help with extra expenses.

Elders and ministers from the congregation stopped by our home to visit and pray with us. Get-well cards and letters flooded our mailbox.

My wonderful colleagues at Freed-Hardeman University stepped in to cover all of my teaching responsibilities for two-plus solid weeks. We couldn't have survived without the compassionate care, emotional support, and hands-on help we received.

§

Blue Task
#10

- Think of someone you know who is about to undergo or has recently undergone a serious surgery.
- Begin by praying for the individual, then purchase and write out a get well card and mail it to them.
- Think of a hands-on way that you may be of practical assistance to the individual. For instance, you may arrange to prepare or purchase a delicious meal for him/her, clean their home, mow their grass, service their vehicle, provide free babysitting, or provide transportation for them or their children.

Chapter Eleven

How to Handle
Worry and Anxiety

"*I seem to worry constantly. Sometimes I even suffer with panic attacks. The anxiety is killing me, but I feel powerless to stop it. What makes matters worse—the more depressed I get, the more anxious I become. That quandary only makes me feel increasingly hopeless. Then I end up feeling guilty as a Christian for worrying so much and not having more faith. It's a vicious cycle and I feel stuck. What am I to do?*"

Frustrating scenarios such as this are not uncommon among persons who suffer with depression. While par for the course, navigating through worry and anxiety can be a real struggle with no simple answers or quick fixes.

§

Diabolical and Deadly Twins

Depression and anxiety form a potentially devastating duo and precarious partnership that wreaks havoc in people's lives. Though not always the case, anxiety disorders often coexist with depression, fueling each other in a downward spiral. Molehills morph into mountains, and we feel afraid, overwhelmed, and hopeless. Irrational fear can certainly incapacitate us if we're not careful.

The poet W. H. Auden aptly called our era the "age of anxiety." Arthur Somers Roche stated, "Anxiety is a thin stream of fear trickling through the mind. If encouraged, it cuts a channel into which all other thoughts are drained." We either feed it or starve it out. Left to its own devices, neurotic worry will completely take over a person's life and swallow them in debilitating despair and dread. Once anxiety gets its unwieldy and intractable tentacles into an individual's psyche and soul, it is difficult to pull it loose so as to disable its harmful effects and reestablish mental and emotional stability.

George Mueller asserts, "The beginning of anxiety is the end of faith, and the beginning of true faith is the end of anxiety." While this may be something of an overstatement, it highlights the perpetual spiritual tension between faith and anxiety. If we're honest with ourselves, we must all admit that we struggle with worry and anxiety at times, though perhaps to differing degrees. It is just part of the human condition. Had Jesus not recognized this reality, he would not have warned against it (Matt. 6:25-34). Untamed anxiousness tends to interfere with our ability to serve others by zapping our energy and holding us hostage. Confronting our fears is necessary in order to put them in their place.

§

Uncertain and Treacherous Terrain

Many scenarios in life have the potential for producing fear and anxiety in us. One of the biggest challenges we face is how to handle anxiety effectively. It's no surprise that, in our society, tranquilizers are so popular and plentiful. Sometimes, the future will naturally appear bleak and threatening. And because of depression's troublesome tendency to distort normal, healthy thought patterns, skew our perceptions, and taint our perspectives, it's not uncommon for a person with melancholy to imagine threats lurking nearby in the shadows, if only figuratively speaking. Those individuals who struggle with full-blown anxiety and various nervous disorders understand this rather unpleasant scenario better than anyone else. It takes the notion of being a proverbial "worry wart" to a whole new level. Depending on your specific flavor of depression, you may or may not relate to this complication.

For some depressives, life seems generally scary and uncertain. It's like there's a bogeyman hiding behind every corner and in every unlit closet. Sometimes, people experience anxiety regarding the outlook or prognosis for their depression itself. It's hard to resist being overcome by worry and fear. Many of my melancholic clients are also confronted with the added hardship of severe panic attacks as well. This situation serves to complicate matters much more.

Various irrational phobias may crop up in extreme conditions such as:

- agoraphobia (fear of crowded places or markets),
- anginophobia (fear of choking),
- amaxophobia (fear of riding in a car or vehicle),
- sito/sitiophobia (fear of food or eating),
- lilapsophobia (fear of tornadoes or hurricanes),
- bacillophobia (fear of microbes),
- verminophobia (fear of germs), or
- polyphobia (fear of many things).

The above list represents just the hem of the garment. The American Psychiatric Association (APA) recognizes more than 100 different phobias. Depressed persons often worry if their depression will be a chronic problem for the rest of their lives. If so, how will they ever survive it? It's sometimes difficult to figure out what's worse: the depression or the anxiety that it often evokes. Either way, both are very hard to get a handle on. So, what are we to do? How should we cope?

§

Things We Worry About

Scripture tells us around 365 times to "fear not" or, in modern English, "don't be afraid." That's both comforting and challenging. These needed words of encouragement ought not to be perceived as a harsh indictment for faithlessness. They are provided to build up and not to tear down. Neither should they be viewed as a quick fix intended to minimize, downplay, or cover up profound anxiety that is being experienced. The very fact that the themes of anxiety and worry are so prevalent in the Bible makes it abundantly clear that people of faith have always struggled with these issues. Lamentably, it is part-and-parcel of our humanity.

As finite, mortal beings, we worry about a myriad of things—relationships, education, career, children, health issues, economics and finances, politics, international affairs, deadlines, spiritual matters, war, and personal safety. Most of the time, these concerns amount to nothing at all in the end. But, in the meantime, we struggle to remain positive. It's all too tempting to habitually run the worst-case scenario in our heads. We become unsettled in the face of various stressors, deal with neurotic nervousness regarding unpredictable situations, and generally deal with a chronic case of anxiety. We even worry about worrying! But there are normal, everyday types of worry on the spectrum versus those severe levels of anxiety that fall in the clinical realm, and everything in between. This reality needs to be fully recognized and acknowledged. Some individuals can't help it that they're chronically anxious due to having a nervous disorder and, therefore, shouldn't be judged as faithless in light of their anxiety problems. It's clearly beyond their control, so we shouldn't unfairly criticize or blame them.

§

Biblical Warriors and "Worriers"

With that disclaimer, the Bible is replete with examples of faithful persons who dealt with issues of anxiety and worry. They struggled just as we struggle with human difficulties in light of unpredictable and precarious circumstances. Yes, again we're in good company!

Abraham and Sarah ached over the absence of a male heir, one God had promised them. Moses fretted about the Hebrews' fragile future as they wandered in the wilderness. Ten of the twelve spies produced widespread panic among the Israelites concerning the "giants" and fortified cities in the Promised Land that stood in the way of securing their inheritance. David feared for his life at the hands of the deranged King Saul, as well as countless other foes. Queen Esther was distressed over the future of the imperiled Jewish people while living in captivity. Elijah was depressed and anxious about the spiritual condition of Israel and his own lack of a protégé to continue his prophetic ministry. John the Baptist grew antsy over whether or not Jesus was indeed the promised Messiah. The apostle Paul was concerned about the spiritual condition of many of his converts on the mission field. Timothy, the young evangelist, apparently struggled with an encumbering case of timidity and personal discouragement. If these heroes of faith struggled, so will we.

§

Blowing Things Out of Proportion

I recently was invited to speak at a church on the topic of depression. Following my presentation, a sweet elderly lady came up and introduced herself to me, confessing she had been dealing with depression for many years. I was touched by her story. She proceeded to share a brilliant practical strategy that she has found to be a lifesaver: "A number of years ago, I decided not to give any real importance to something that wouldn't matter one hundred years from now. That has eliminated many of my problems." I believe that's sage advice and think we ought to name it, *The One-Hundred-Year Rule*. If we evaluate our concern and determine that it won't amount to a hill of beans after we're dead and gone, what's the point in worrying about it or even giving it the time of day? It's a waste of our all-too-brief precious time here on earth.

§

The Problem of Anxiety and the Divine Remedy

Anxiety sets us on edge. It produces uncertainty concerning the present and future. It makes us question our basic belief system. It sucks our emotional and spiritual energy dry like the potent gravitational vortex of a black hole. It keeps us awake at night tossing and turning and causes us to make rash decisions and act irrationally. It confounds our logic, consumes our minds, and clouds our vision. Yes, anxiety presents a formidable problem. The Lord evidently understood this reality with great clarity. In Matthew 6:25-30, 34 (ESV), Jesus says:

> [25]"Therefore I tell you, do not be anxious about your life, what you will eat or what you will drink, nor about your body, what you will put on. Is not life more than food, and the body more than clothing?[26] Look at the birds of the air: they neither sow nor reap nor gather into barns, and yet your heavenly Father feeds them. Are you not of more value than they?[27] And which of you by being anxious can add a single hour to his span of life?[28] And why are you anxious about clothing? Consider the lilies of the field, how they grow: they neither toil nor spin,[29] yet I tell you, even Solomon in all his glory was not arrayed like one of these.[30] But if God so clothes the grass of the field, which today is alive and tomorrow is thrown into the oven, will he not much more clothe you, O you of little faith? . . .[34] Therefore

do not be anxious about tomorrow, for tomorrow will be anxious for itself. Sufficient for the day is its own trouble."

Jesus's teaching reminds us of God's tender care for all creation, even the tiniest of birds, which are not nearly as valuable in his eyes as we are. If God takes care of the sparrow, surely, he will see after our needs, too! Jesus tells us that worrying about things beyond our control is pointless and certainly won't extend the longevity of our lives. Since our Heavenly Father personally attends to the survival and seasonal flowering of the lilies and grass of the field, surely, he will more so clothe us in warmth and splendor.

It's comforting to realize that God already knows what we need before we ever speak a word (see Matthew 6:8, 32). He is omniscient, but still desires that we recognize and acknowledge our complete dependence upon him for every blessing and need. "Every good and every perfect gift is from above, coming down from the Father of lights with whom there is no variation or shadow due to change" (James 1:17, ESV). Worrying only further complicates our situation and makes things worse. We can and should trust God to take care of us. But every one of us, at times, struggles to relinquish our illusion of control.

§

A wise person once told me that we should only focus on those things that are within our control, but avoid worrying about those things that fall outside the parameters of our meager might. We are feeble and frail. Our power is puny. Psalm 103:14 (ESV) states, "For he knows our frame; he remembers that we are dust." There is only so much we can do.

It's important to remember our own limitations to prevent ourselves from becoming prideful and arrogant, let alone delusional. It is sobering to recognize that our lives are but "a mist that appears for a little time and then vanishes" (James 4:14b,

ESV). When we come to the full realization that the world and everything in it belongs to our omnipotent Creator, and that it's totally at his disposal, we'll be more apt to relinquish our worries. This requires faith, trust, and courage.

§

Divine Comfort from God's Promises

God's Word supplies us with much-needed comfort. In Philippians 4:6-7 (ESV), Paul writes: "Do not be anxious about anything, but in everything by prayer and supplication with thanksgiving let your requests be made known to God. And the peace of God, which surpasses all understanding, will guard your hearts and your minds in Christ Jesus." Anxiety may thus be counteracted through a prayerful and grateful spirit. We are reminded in this beautiful scripture that we're not all alone in this world and that God cares deeply about us, no matter the situation.

When we take full advantage of our twenty-four-hour hotline to God through prayer, we can rest assured that he is listening to us and is willing and able to help. Even though our circumstances don't always necessarily change dramatically or improve instantly, the peace of God is something we can expect in our lives rather than always an immediate answer. This is a divine promise.

Knowing that we have Christ as a sympathetic high priest interceding for us in heaven, Hebrews 4:16 (ESV) exclaims, "Let us then with confidence draw near to the throne of grace, that we may receive mercy and find grace to help in time of need." God is totally trustworthy, and he loves you. He promises to help you. He only wants the best in your life. Notice how we are encouraged to confidently and boldly enter into God's loving presence and come before his throne of grace? Now that's cause for comfort and hope!

When I was a child growing up on the mission-field in South Africa, there was a song we used to sing in Sunday school that has always stuck with me. The words went as follows:

Why worry when you can pray?
Trust in Jesus, for he will lead the way!
Don't be a doubting Thomas,
Just lean upon his promise.
Why worry, worry, worry, worry
When you can pray?
(author unknown)

Since we know the Lord is on our side, it simply doesn't make sense to waste valuable time and energy fretting about the uncertain future. The future belongs to God and he is in control of it. Proverbs 12:25 (ESV) says, "Anxiety in a man's heart weighs him down, but a good word makes him glad." Worry never got anyone anywhere, but prayer will get us home.

§

Staying Present-Focused Rather Than Future-Focused

It's important to live one day at a time. When we get out too far ahead of ourselves, we're borrowing trouble from tomorrow. We build up imaginary and hypothetical scenarios in our minds of what might happen to us and those we love. In doing this, we begin to fret and wring our hands in anxiety about things that have not yet come to pass and possibly may never transpire at all. Our focus becomes our reality.

Anxiety grows and multiplies by our preoccupation on potential threats, whether real or imaginary. It subsides, however, when we refocus our minds on something else, such as serving or helping others. It's a good distraction that breaks our unhealthy (and often irrational) train of thought. In Matthew

6:34, Jesus tells us that it is both foolish and futile to squander today worrying about tomorrow. All we have at our disposal is now, so let's remain focused on positive and life-enriching things.

Philippians 4:8 (ESV) says, "Finally, brothers, whatever is true, whatever is honorable, whatever is just, whatever is pure, whatever is lovely, whatever is commendable, if there is any excellence, if there is anything worthy of praise, think about these things." Train your mind to meditate on those things that are uplifting, inspiring, and hope-full. When we're focused on meaningful, compassionate service, we have less of a tendency to waste our available energy resources on worry. This is where a thought interruption and replacement technique can come into play as a helpful strategy to turn the tide.

§

Thought-Stopping Technique

The following exercise is a counseling method I frequently use with anxiety-ridden and obsessive-compulsive clients. The technique is called "Thought Stopping," and it originates from Cognitive Behavioral Therapy (CBT). Here is a simple step-by-step outline for you to follow:

Step One: Get a pen and paper and make two columns. At the top of the left-hand column write the following heading: "Unhealthy and Unhelpful Thoughts." Below jot down three or four negative and/or irrational thoughts that you tend to fixate on. Condense each of these ideas into a sentence or two for the sake of simplicity and clarity.

Step Two: At the top of the right-hand column, write the following heading: "Positive Thought Replacements." Now beside each of the negative thoughts located in the left-hand column, think of more healthy, accurate, and positive replacements. Jot down three such alternate (or reframed) thoughts in the right-hand column to counter each negative thought. These may include, among other things, themes related to serving others well.

Step Three: Read the negative thoughts out loud, one at a time, and immediately follow up by reading the positive replacement sentences. Repeat this step until you have each of them committed to memory. (It may be beneficial to tackle one negative thought at time to simplify this process.) Once you have memorized each of your positive replacements, proceed to the next step.

Step Four: Close your eyes and take a few deep breaths. Inhale through your nose, and exhale slowly out your mouth with a whooshing sound. Do this for approximately one minute, allowing yourself to enter into a more relaxed state. Try to cleanse your mind of all thoughts.

Step Five: Focus on the first of the negative thoughts, repeating it in your mind several times for about forty-five seconds. Pay close attention to each and every word.

Step Six: In your mind shout, "STOP!" as loudly as you can. You may also choose to visualize a big stop sign, red flashing warning lights, or even imagine a nuclear alarm siren blaring over the airwaves. (It's helpful to practice this step prior to starting the exercise.) Once you have done this, rid your head of all thoughts and allow your mind to go completely blank for fifty to sixty seconds. If the negative thought (or any other thought for that matter) creeps back in, holler "STOP!" once more and force your mind to go blank. The goal here is to gain control over the negative thought. Once you have successfully managed to blank all thoughts out of your mind for roughly one minute, you will be ready to move on to the next step.

Step Seven: Rehearse your positive replacement thoughts in your mind, repeating them with conviction a number of times in sequence. Do this for at least ninety seconds or so. Allow these more rational and uplifting thoughts or ideas to supplant the negative, irrational thoughts.

Repeat the entire process for each of the negative thoughts that have formerly plagued your mind, causing you anxiety and duress. Practice this technique twice per day in a quiet place.

Many counselees report that by using the thought-stopping method, they have managed to gain greater control over their unhealthy, irrational, and anxiety provoking thought patterns. It is a liberating experience for them and can be for you, too.

§

Being Stuck in the Past

Another pitfall to avoid is dwelling upon yesterday's mistakes, failures, and disappointments. Fixating on the past keeps us from living fully in the present. It throws us off track and is counterproductive, saps our energy, undermines our confidence, and bogs us down. In Philippians 3:13b-14 (ESV), Paul writes, "forgetting what lies behind and straining forward to what lies ahead, I press on toward the goal for the prize of the upward call of God in Christ Jesus." Paul didn't allow his past mistakes and regrets to distract him from his present ministry. He couldn't afford to. Neither should we succumb to this treacherous trap. There's too much at stake for us and those we love.

As Christians, one of the greatest blessings we possess is God's ongoing forgiveness and perpetual grace, which continually covers us and removes our sin. We can start each day afresh, being made new and clean on the inside. Let go of the burden of guilt that weighs you down and walk in the spiritual freedom and wholeness that Christ provides (see 1 John 1:7-9). I often remind believers who struggle with various addictions of Paul's encouraging words in 2 Corinthians 5:17 (ESV): "Therefore, if anyone is in Christ, he is a new creation. The old has passed away; behold, the new has come." What a wonderful word of encouragement! The old has passed and the new is come. God offers us another chance to live fully and victoriously for him. It simply doesn't get any better than that.

When anxiety takes over, we forget His promises, underestimate His power, and are blinded to His presence. Perceived threats from the outside cause us to default into survival mode. Sometimes, the anxiety and worry make us lash out in anger and frustration, most often toward those who love us. The very ones we need by our side, we drive away. It is our unhealthy, maladaptive way of coping, rather than handing our anxieties over to God.

§

Peter: Relinquishing Control to the Lord

The way up is the way down—the path of humility. First Peter 5:6-7 (ESV) says: "Humble yourselves, therefore, under the mighty hand of God so that at the proper time he may exalt you, casting all your anxieties on him, because he cares for you." Letting go of our pride and releasing our cares to the Lord is challenging to do. Peter knew this from personal experience. We tend to be control freaks. It's difficult for us to trust God fully and rely on him completely. The most important phrase for us to focus on in the above verse is the last one, "because he cares for you." Understanding the depth of God's incomparable loving care and compassion bolsters our confidence and courage. It supplies spiritual hope and joy to our lives, even when in the midst of the most threatening storms that rage around and within us.

Do you remember the story, in Matthew 14, of how the disciples saw Jesus walking on the Sea of Galilee at night? Peter asked permission to come out to Jesus. Jesus said, "Come!" So, without a second thought, Peter climbed out of his boat and started walking to Jesus on the water. Initially, Peter's confidence was running high because his focus was fixed on the Lord. His spiritual confidence was placed in the right person—the Lord, and not himself. However, the instant he got distracted, took his eyes off Jesus, and started giving heed to the winds and the waves around him, his confidence evaporated. He began to sink. Jesus had to reach out his hand to rescue Peter from drowning in the brink. It was a hard and humiliating lesson to learn. Peter was forced to eat a big ol' slice of humble pie. In a way, we've all been there before—time and again. Our faith frequently flounders, but God's love for us will never fail.

Yes, most of us can relate well to Peter's on-again, off-again faith struggles. One moment we're walking on water with Jesus, the next we're sinking into a sea of despair. Like Peter, we lose our focus and forget where our strength really lies, in the Lord, not us. Our long-term recollection of God's proven track record is inadequate. We also have a short attention span in the now. That's why the storm raging around us tends to get the better of us. We're too easily distracted and dismayed by the "winds" and the "waves" of worry, fear, and doubt. So, we suffer the natural consequences. We must regain our focus, keeping our eyes firmly fixed on Jesus, the author and perfecter of our faith (Heb. 12:2).

§

God is Bigger Than Your Greatest Fears

It is comforting to know that no matter how big our problems or perceived threats to our security may seem to us, our Almighty

God is far bigger and stronger. He is the omnipotent Creator of heaven and earth who made us in his own image, who knows us intimately, and loves us beyond our comprehension. Thank goodness we don't have to rely on our own meager strength to survive this life emotionally or otherwise. Our strength comes from the Lord.

Psalm 121 is a beautiful "Song of Ascents" that the Jewish pilgrims used to joyfully sing as they ascended Mount Zion into the Holy City of Jerusalem for their annual feasts. Its inspired words are truly uplifting to the soul.

121   A SONG OF ASCENTS
I lift up my eyes to the hills.
From where does my help come?
2   My help comes from the Lord,
who made heaven and earth.
3   He will not let your foot be moved;
he who keeps you will not slumber.
4   Behold, he who keeps Israel
will neither slumber nor sleep.
5   The Lord is your keeper;
the Lord is your shade on your right hand.
6   The sun shall not strike you by day,
nor the moon by night.
7   The Lord will keep you from all evil;
he will keep your life.
8   The Lord will keep
your going out and your coming in
from this time forth and forevermore.

As believers, we are invited by Christ to cast all our cares and anxieties upon him, our heavenly Father who is willing and able to help us in our times of distress and fear. Those who suffer with chronic levels of anxiety and worry may find spiritual peace, rest, and solace within the safe haven of God's love and grace. The Lord of heaven and earth will never let your foot slip. He will never fall asleep on his watch. He will be your shade and shelter by day and night. He will hold you close to his bosom and keep you from harm. Never doubt his deep and abiding love for you, his beloved child. Fear not, for your heavenly Father is with you always.

§

Blue Task
#11

- Write down a list of the top ten things that you most worry about.
- Once you've written the list, read it out loud.
- Now, give the list over to God by casting all your cares on the Lord, telling him that you no longer wish to carry these burdens alone (see 1 Pet. 5:7).
- Next, either burn, shred, or tear up the list of your worries and anxieties to symbolize your letting it go.
- Practice my thought-stopping exercise and follow the instructions closely on pg. 100. (Note: there is also a video tutorial on RyanNoelFraser.com located on the "Blues Video Resources" page.

Chapter Twelve

Good Company

THERE'S a tendency for depressed persons to feel isolated, like nobody else grasps what they're going though. Being lonely is a painful experience. However, spiritual comfort and support are found in good company. Pastor Nick Honerkamp states it this way: "The definition of a friendship is a relationship with no agenda." God sets the lonely in spiritual families (Psalm 68:6). Where would we be without our friends? I dare not venture to imagine such a solitary world.

§

A friend in need is a friend indeed! This well-known adage is one that most of us are familiar with. When the going gets rough and times are tough, we typically find out who our real friends are. One of my most cherished friendships is with John, a Christian man who is several years older than me. Come to think of it, he is pretty ancient—perhaps as old as Methuselah (I love you, John!). We originally got to know each other more than twenty-five years ago when I served as his youngest child's youth minister. Since then, despite the miles that separate us, we consistently check in with each other via telephone and email, and we occasionally get to spend time with one another in person during short visits. Our friendship has deepened, matured, and become more meaningful to both of us over the years. With the passing of time, we have come to refer to each other as "foul-weather friends" or just "foul friends." The reason for this term of endearment is we know just about everything there is to know about one another, yet still love and respect each other anyway. We have made a covenant to always tell one another the truth about what is going on behind the scenes in our private, personal lives, thereby providing ongoing mutual support and spiritual accountability. We have both promised to do this no matter how embarrassing or uncomfortable it might make us feel at times. All we have to say is, "How are you doing lately?" and that is code for, "Who have you been when nobody has been watching?" We have both seen the other go through some pretty bumpy stretches, but we have remained constant and faithful companions who are committed to our relationship. Authentic friendship like this is something that is rare and difficult to come by.

§

I can honestly say that I have been extremely blessed to have a number of close, trustworthy Christian friends over the years, ones whom I can rely upon no matter the circumstances. They are there for me whenever I need their help, and I pray that I am there for them, too. Winnie the Pooh once said to his dear friend, Christopher Robin, "If you live to be a hundred, I want to live to be a hundred minus one day, so I never have to live without you."[4] We can all work on becoming better friends.

---

4   The Trustees of the Pooh Properties. Pooh's Little Instruction Book. New York: Dutton Children's Books, 1995. (Note: while the book credits A.A. Milne as inspiring the quote, he did not author this work or the particular quote for that matter. The original quote by Milne in The House at Pooh Corner (ch. 10) is significantly different: "Pooh, promise you won't forget about me, ever. Not even when I'm a hundred." Pooh thought for a little. "How old shall I be then?" "Ninety-nine." Pooh nodded. "I promise," he said.)

The fellowship and companionship provided by meaningful friendship is a priceless commodity. Albert Camus (1913–1960), French author, journalist, and philosopher, once wrote, "Don't walk behind me; I may not lead. Don't walk in front of me; I may not follow. Just walk beside me and be my friend."

Unfortunately, people to whom we give our trust occasionally let us down. This results in us becoming suspicious of people and their underlying motives. Once a so-called friend has burned you, it makes it more difficult to open up to others out of fear of being hurt again. We can go into defensive mode and build emotional walls around ourselves that keep others out, trying to insulate ourselves from the vulnerability and pain that stems from relationships that go awry. The Prodigal Son (Luke 15:11-32) seemed to have fair-weather friends who were "takers" rather than "givers," because when he ran out of money, he ran out of friends. They quickly vanished when he needed them the most. He was left destitute, having to survive by himself in horrible conditions. Sitting in absolute squalor, the pig slop even began to look appetizing.

§

Although the Native Americans had no written alphabet prior to meeting the white European explorers, their language was far from primitive or inadequate. The vocabulary of many Indian tribal people was as broad and expansive as that of their French and English counterparts, if not more eloquent and expressive. For example, their special term for the word "friend" was actually a short descriptive phrase: "One-who-carries-my-sorrows-on-his-back." What a beautiful sentiment!

As Christians we need to work hard at becoming reliable and trustworthy friends to others. Galatians 6:2 (ESV) says, "Bear one another's burdens, and so fulfill the law of Christ." Jesus modeled for his disciples (and us) how to be a true friend. During his earthly ministry, he was often criticized by the scribes and Pharisees for the type of company he chose to keep. In Matthew 11:19 (ESV), Jesus says, "The Son of Man came eating and drinking, and they say, 'Look at him! A glutton and a drunkard, a friend of tax collectors and sinners!' Yet wisdom is justified by her deeds." For Christ, companionship was always a means to an end, never an end in and of itself. He had a deep, eternal spiritual purpose for it, in that it served as a vehicle whereby he built connections to individuals in order to draw them closer to God.

§

Throughout history there have been inspirational examples of true friendship. Around the year 1490, there were two best friends, Albrecht Dürer and Franz Knigstein. They were both starving artists living in Nuremberg, a city-state in the German state of Bavaria. Since each of them was dirt poor, they had to work odd jobs to support themselves while they studied fine art. But their labor took a great deal of their time, making artistic advancement slow. Eventually they came to the conclusion that something had to give, so they made a solemn pact with each other. They drew straws to decide which one would work to support them both while the other focused all his energies on art. Albrecht won the luck of the draw, while his good friend worked tirelessly at hard manual labor to put bread on the table. The plan was that when Albrecht became successful, he would then support Franz as he studied art.

Traveling to the great cultural centers of Europe to grow in his craft, Albrecht eventually became successful, and he returned home to honor his promise to Franz. But Albrecht quickly recognized the heavy price his friend had paid. Due to hard manual labor, Franz's fingers had become arthritic. No longer could he execute the delicate brush strokes required for fine painting. Although his artistic dreams had been shattered, he never expressed bitterness but only joy in his friend's success.

One day, Albrecht discovered Franz kneeling with his twisted and gnarled fingers intertwined in prayer, quietly beseeching God to bring additional success to his friend. Dürer, the great artistic genius, hurriedly sketched the folded hands of his best friend and later completed a truly great masterpiece, known today as The Praying Hands.

Art galleries throughout the world feature Albrecht Dürer's amazing art, and this particular masterpiece continues to tell a beautiful story of love, sacrifice, and gratitude. It has served as a powerful reminder for people for more than five centuries that they may also discover comfort, courage, and strength in the Lord. If it weren't for the special, sacrificial friendship that existed between Franz and Albrecht, the world would not be blessed by the powerful and inspiring image of The Praying Hands.

§

A faithful companion is one who can be counted on when the chips are down. Chapter 20 of 1 Samuel describes the beautiful friendship of David and Jonathan. Even when his own demented father, King Saul, tried to pin David to the wall with his spear out of frenzied jealousy, Jonathan remained a loyal friend. He literally saved David's life by secretly warning him to run and hide from the royal wrath. Jonathan made an everlasting covenant with the house of David and made David swear his love for him, "for he loved him as he loved his own soul."[5] Later, at their touching farewell for the sake of David's safety, the Bible says, "And they kissed one another and wept with one another, David weeping the most. Then Jonathan said to David, 'Go in peace, because we have sworn both of us in the name of the LORD,' saying, 'The LORD shall be between me and you, and between my offspring and your offspring, forever.'"[6]

---

5   1 Sam. 20:17, ESV.
6   1 Sam. 20:41b-42, ESV.

Their relationship remained meaningful to both of them and sustained them through difficult times.

After Jonathan was slain in battle at the hands of the ferocious Philistines[7] and Saul had committed suicide by falling on his own sword,[8] David eventually came to power. When he sat upon the throne in Jerusalem, he was completely faithful to his promise to Jonathan and cared for his friend's son Mephibosheth, who was crippled in both feet. David restored all the land to him that had formerly belonged to his grandfather Saul. Mephibosheth was also given a permanent place of honor at David's dinner table for the rest of his life.[9] David's special friendship with Jonathan thus persisted even in death.

§

Proverbs 27:10 (ESV) states, "Do not forsake your friend and your father's friend, and do not go to your brother's house in the day of your calamity. Better is a neighbor who is near than a brother who is far away." Most of my adult life during the better part of my twenties, thirties, and forties, I was geographically separated from my flesh-and-blood family by many miles. This has forced me to rely heavily upon the companionship of not only my sweet wife but also that of good Christian friends in whatever location my family has been living at the time.

In more recent years, I've developed some close friendships with a group of guys who love to go hiking together, usually a couple of times per year. We proudly call ourselves The North Jackson Hiking Association. Our sarcastic slogan used to be, "No man left behind." That was, of course, until we accidently left a guy behind (a state trooper friend of ours, mind you), sleeping in his hammock one sub-freezing morning while the

---

7   See 1 Sam. 31:2; 1 Chron. 10:2.
8   See 1 Sam. 31:4; 1 Chron. 10:4-5.
9   See 2 Sam. 9:1-13.

rest of us hastily broke camp, packed up our gear, and hiked several miles back to our warm vehicles. When we realized he was missing from the group, we were all more than a little concerned. He had no map, no CB, and no cell-phone service, as we were in a remote, mountainous region of Virginia (Mt. Rogers to be precise). To our great relief, over an hour later, when he eventually found his way back to the parking lot where we were anxiously waiting in our heated cars, all he said was, "Let me give you guys some advice: In future, count your people before you leave camp!" He definitely wasn't charmed at the time, and for good reason. Sorry about that, Jeff, though in retrospect it makes for a pretty hilarious story! And, he's a good sport.

Along the rugged mountain trails, we trek, and in the primitive campsites where we pitch our tents and hang our hammocks, we share in uplifting Christian fellowship. Men in particular crave this kind of "male bonding" that takes place around a campfire late at night where the protective walls come down and we no longer feel isolated from one another. A popular saying among our group is: "What happens on the trail, stays on the trail!" One of Satan's most effective strategies with men is to divide and conquer. He uses machismo, competitiveness, and isolation to prevent mutual support and accountability and makes us feel like we are drifting along through life without any real moorings or stability. Those of us who struggle with depression especially need godly fellowship, emotional support, and encouragement.

Embarking on our hiking trips is a much-needed escape from the "dog-eat-dog" world of work and from the frenzied pace of life that many of us experience on a daily basis. We are able to commune with God, nature, and one another. For those of us who are married, our wives seem more than happy for us to be gone for a few days because they know we will return rejuvenated and reenergized as husbands and fathers. And, yes, after a few days away from my creature comforts and family, I do begin missing home, which we all-too-easily can take for granted if we aren't careful.

§

"Duct Tape" and Me

During the first weekend of November 2010, our hiking group took an unforgettable trip to the Great Smoky Mountains National Park in East Tennessee. We had been planning for several months to summit "Rocky Top" on the Appalachian Trail (AT), hiking up from Cades Cove. As the day approached, the weather reports were looking more and more unfavorable, with the threat of an early winter storm and the possibility of mid-twenty-degree temperatures and six to eight inches of snow. Being the rough-and-tough guys we are (okay, that's a gross overstatement!), we ill-advisedly thought we would go anyway, so we did. There were around fourteen of us in our party. I was especially excited to go because I had been slaving day and night on my doctoral dissertation, and, boy, did I need a break!

When we arrived at the trailhead in the early afternoon, it was raining pretty steadily but not terribly cold outside, which was a plus, so we put on our ponchos and gaiters, snapped some quick group photos, and hit the trail. Due to group-size restrictions, the plan was for half of us to spend the night at a backcountry campsite with the other half going on up to Russell Field Shelter for the night. We planned to meet up the next day and hike along the AT to Spence Field and then over to Rocky Top.

As with all of our hikes, adrenaline was running high, especially with our awareness of the potential for inclement weather. As we began our slow ascent, I noticed how the rain gradually started turning to slush and then snow as we gained altitude. By the time we reached the campsite to drop off the first party, the ground was completely covered. My group knew that we were burning daylight and needed to get up the mountain pronto, so as the "Trailblazer" (my given trail name), I kicked it into high gear. God gave me skinny chicken-legs, but along with them thankfully came speed and stamina—something which I've sort of reveled in over the years.

Before long, the gradual incline turned steep and the trail became increasingly more rugged, treacherous, and slick. Snow kept falling and by now the flakes had the magical appearance of giant cotton balls as they floated gracefully to the ground obscuring visibility. The sight was absolutely spectacular to behold, especially accentuated by the near to surreal silence that accompanied it. All you could hear were the abnormally large snowflakes landing upon the alpine forest's trees and ground cover below.

After about three miles of trudging along, we were all growing fatigued, and each stride and breath became increasingly more difficult. And that's when I hit a wall like I never had before while hiking or haven't since. My entire body ached from lugging my overstuffed backpack and my legs felt like they were on fire. Physically, psychologically, and emotionally I was spent—completely finished. I simply couldn't take another step and took my two walking sticks and planted them in a snow bank.

"Guys, I need to stop. I want you to go on, but I've got to take a load off for a minute or two and catch a breather," I said.

"We can wait with you, Trailblazer. It's not a problem."

"No, I want you guys to keep going. I'll catch up eventually."

"You sure?" said someone. "We're happy to wait for you."

My pride was hurt. Nobody ever waited on me on the trail. I was usually the one leading the pack. "Yes, I'm sure. Please go on."

"Okay, we'll see you on up ahead."

"All right. Good luck!" said one of the guys and they started up the path once more.

I was struggling to get enough oxygen into my lungs, so I pulled off my backpack, took out my trusty blue tarp to cover myself, and plopped down on the trail. I was *done*. Finito.

That's where Adam (aka "Duct Tape"), a newbie to our group who had been standing back silently, spoke up.

"Hey, Trailblazer, I'm just going to sit under the tarp with you and keep you company," he said in his laid back, charming Southern accent. He didn't ask permission. "I could stand to take a bit of a breather, too." Removing his backpack, he sat down beside me on the trail, stretching his long, lanky legs out in front of him. We just sat there in silent solitude for a moment, then he broke the silence and made some small talk about the beauty of the snowfall and our spectacular surroundings. I don't think he really had any idea, at the time, just how much I needed his kind and nonjudgmental support in that moment or how much his positive attitude and encouraging words meant to me. We must have sat there for fifteen to twenty minutes as the snow pelted us and quickly covered the tarp with a white, frosty blanket.

After resting for a good while, I finally began to catch my second wind.

"I'm feeling better," I said. "I think I'm ready to press on."

"You sure? We can sit here longer if you need to."

"Yes, I think I'm ready to get going."

"All right," Duct Tape replied. "Let's do this t-h-a-n-g!"

We managed to pick ourselves up off the ground, put on our backpacks again, and slowly but surely wound our way up the mountain switchbacks toward the elusive shelter near the crest. In fact, we eventually managed to catch up with the other five guys who had gone on ahead of us and who, by now, looked thoroughly exhausted themselves.

By the time our band of seven brothers reached the shelter that evening at dusk, there were nine to ten inches of snow on the ground and the temperature had plummeted into the upper teens. But with the warm companionship of each other and the help of a toasty, crackling fire, we survived to tell the tale. And it seems to only get better (and more exaggerated) each time we tell it!

§

Building and strengthening our friendships is something that requires intentionality, significant effort, and time. Men and women alike need close same-sex friends who can serve as a valuable support network and ongoing source of encouragement and accountability. A godly companion is someone who is willing to tell you the truth about yourself.

Often, we struggle to be objective when it comes to evaluating ourselves, for we all have blind spots. True friends care about the eternal destiny of one another's souls. Therefore, they are prepared to confront each other in love and awaken each other up to the hidden, insidious dangers of sin, the first step leading to repentance and reconciliation with God. Proverbs 27:5-6 (ESV) says, "Better is open rebuke than hidden love. Faithful are the wounds of a friend; profuse are the kisses of an enemy." Genuine and authentic friends will tell us things we need to hear—but don't want to—things that are not necessarily easy or pleasant for them to say. This is especially true since we often avoid constructive criticism and don't like having "reality checks." But godly companions are always there for us when we need them the most, not necessarily when we want them around. These types of friends have our best interest at heart. We have heard it said before that, "People don't care how much you know, until they know how much you care." While the truth often hurts at first, it is always best in the long run. I am reminded of how Paul confronted Peter with the truth about his hypocrisy when it came to avoiding table fellowship with Gentiles whenever his Jewish friends were in town (Gal. 2:11-21; 6:1-2). Nathan confronted David with the ugly truth regarding the secret sin of his adulterous relationship with Bathsheba and his murderous plot against her innocent husband, Uriah (2 Sam. 12:1-13). A true friend is a person who knows your faults and flaws but loves you all the same. The familiar maxim goes something like, "Hate the sin, but love the sinner." Christ loves us, despite our sin, although he certainly doesn't condone it. Romans 5:8 (NIV) states, "But God demonstrates his own love for us in this: While we were still sinners, Christ died for us."

As faithful companions, it is our duty to help our friends walk on the straight and narrow and do what is right in God's sight. However, we must also be there for them when they suffer the painful consequences of their sin, so that we can help them pick up the pieces, regroup, and start afresh. Loyal friends never say, "I told you so!" They extend mercy, grace, forgiveness, and encouragement, rather than ridicule or self-righteousness. They believe in us and give us the benefit of the doubt as they extend patience our way. We must allow people the room to make their own mistakes. Genuine love is demonstrated when you consistently love a person in spite of their errors. It has been said that if you really want to know who your friends are, just make a mistake!

A true friend is also an individual who puts your needs ahead of his or her own. Jesus was and is a true friend. He knew from the beginning that he was going to have to lay down his own life for the world. In John 10:14-15 (ESV), Christ states, "I am the good shepherd. I know my own and my own know me, just as the Father knows me and I know the Father; and I lay down my life for the sheep." Later on, he says, "This is my commandment, that you love one another as I have loved you. Greater love has no one than this, that someone lays down his life for his friends" (John 15:12-13, ESV).

Jesus developed a different kind of relationship with his disciples than that of the dynamic between a master and his servants. Jesus called them his "friends" (v. 15). By taking our eyes off ourselves and by focusing them on the needs and concerns of others, we can actually find self-worth and purpose in our lives. If you want friends, be a friend! Companionship is a wonderful gift from God. We need close relationships with others to remain emotionally healthy and happy. There must be people in our lives whom we can feel safe opening up to and sharing our burdens with and vice versa. These are people who will lend us a listening ear and understanding during the tough times. They rejoice with us when we rejoice, and they mourn with us when we mourn (Rom. 12:15).

§

If we get a little creative, we can use the word "FRIEND" as an acronym, employing each of the letters to stand for various important qualities of true friendship.

True friends are Forever. The Bible says, "A friend loves at all times, and a brother is born for adversity" (Prov. 17:17, ESV).

True friends keep it Real. They speak the truth in love (Eph. 4:15) and don't let us easily off the hook when we are clearly in the wrong.

They are genuinely Interested in us. They want to know what is going on in our lives. They want to be aware of any personal struggles we are facing, so that they can be sensitive to our needs and make supplications to God for us. They want to be able to share in not only our joys but also our sorrows (Rom. 12:15).

Legitimate friends are Empathetic. They want to be able to see the world from our vantage point and through our eyes. They do their best to put themselves in our shoes. When we hurt, they hurt. They lend us a shoulder to lean on and even cry on if need be.

Good friends are Near. They are there when we need them the most (Prov. 27:10). They remain emotionally and physically available to us.

Finally, true friends are Dedicated. In other words, they are loyal to our relationship and committed to making it stronger and deeper with the passing of time. Real friends honor our decisions. They stick by us through thick and thin, good and bad. They trust us and, therefore, always give us the benefit of the doubt. They will go out on a limb for us.

True and godly companions are not easily found. They are definitely a blessing from above, so never take your true friends for granted, and work diligently on becoming a better, faithful, and true companion yourself. Be a friend to others just as Jesus has been a true friend to you. The wise man once wrote, "A man of many companions may come to ruin, but there is a friend who sticks closer than a brother" (Prov. 18:24). Jesus is that kind of friend. He has proven his love and commitment to us time and time again.

Someone has said, "A real friend is one who walks in when the rest of the world walks out." The real question is, then, what kind of friend am I? Am I someone who can be trusted? Someone who is reliable and can be counted on? Someone who is prepared to lay down his life for the sake of his friends? Jesus did. He is our absolutely best friend and taught us how to offer the precious gift of companionship to others.

If you want to have good friends, the first rule of thumb is to be a good friend to others. The gift of meaningful friendship began with Christ and continues with you. Reach out to a friend you've been neglecting of late or develop a new friendship with someone who seems they could use a good companion.

§

Blue Task
#12

- Prayerfully select an acquaintance of yours that you may wish to befriend at a deeper level.
- Reach out to that individual and invite them out for dinner or some other activity to get to know them better.
- Alternatively, you may also choose to reach out to a longtime friend with whom you've lost contact over the years. Check up on them to see how they're doing. All you need to do is let them know you've recently been thinking about them, praying for them, and wondering how they have been doing.

Chapter Thirteen

The Power of Laughter

I love hanging out with my wife, Missy. She always knows how to tickle my funny bone with her corny jokes, like this one: "What does corn say when you give it a compliment? Aw, shucks!" Since she was born in Independence, Kansas, and raised in a house located right beside a large cornfield, there's no doubt that she was corn-fed. Honestly, my kids will blow my pretend "cool" cover by testifying that I really can't say anything, because I am the unrivaled King of Corniness. Thankfully, my family puts up with my dry sense of humor anyway, sometimes with audible groans of agony at my knee-slapping one-liners.

Here are a few corny jokes I like for your punny amusement or agony, just depending on your particular sense of humor:

- Why did the Clydesdale give the pony a glass of water? Because he was a little horse.
- What's the difference between the bird flu and the swine flu? One requires *tweetment* and the other an *oinkment*.
- What's brown and sticky? A stick. (I particularly like that one.)
- What did the policeman say to his belly button? You're under a vest.
- What do you call a pig that does karate? A pork chop.

- What did the yoga instructor say when her landlord tried to evict her? Namaste.
- What do you call birds that stick together? Vel-crows.
- What did the ocean say to the shore? Nothing, it just waved.
- Why did the golfer bring two pairs of pants? In case he got a hole in one.
- Why don't melons get married? Because they cantaloupe.
- What do lawyers wear to work? Lawsuits.
- Which side of a duck has the most feathers? The outside.
- What did the fisherman say to the magician? Pick a cod, any cod.

§

Laughter is good medicine. No, seriously!

Have you ever wondered if God has a sense of humor? Since we're all made in God's image, I believe it's safe to say that he does, and a great one at that. Humor is part of our divinely created nature. Even infants are able to smile and laugh when barely a few months old. It's a natural instinct God has put into the human species. Isn't it an amazing thing to consider? What a great blessing!

To recognize God's inherent, avid sense of humor, all you have to do is check out some of the funny and bizarre-looking creatures God made for his and our sheer enjoyment. Ever seen a proboscis monkey, mantis shrimp, hooded seal, Komondor dog, Angora rabbit, emperor tamarin, pink fairy armadillo, axolotl (or ajolote), aye-aye, tarsier, frill-necked lizard, or one of my personal favorites—the blobfish? You can't help but smile or laugh out loud when beholding these funny-looking creatures. Their appearance is truly funny and rather entertaining. Or what about the more familiar hippopotamus, sloth, or ostrich? They too are absolutely hilarious animals. God apparently had tons of fun designing and creating each of them. I can just hear it now:

God hollers, "Hey guys, you're not gonna believe this one!" Just then the entire angelic host in heaven spontaneously erupts into raucous laughter.

Proverbs 15:13 (ESV) says, "A glad heart makes a cheerful face, but by sorrow of heart the spirit is crushed." Then Proverbs 17:22 (ESV) asserts, "A joyful heart is good medicine, but a crushed spirit dries up the bones." Of all the people in the world, Christians ought to exhibit the most unbridled joy and laughter. After all, we have so much to be thankful for. However, I could swear that some believers were weaned on lemons, or at least dill pickles! They are veritable sourpusses who can be a real bummer to be around. It's almost as if they're afraid that if they dare to smile—let alone crack a joke—their face might just shatter in pieces. That's sad. Whatever happened to the abundant life?

§

There are several noteworthy benefits to developing a healthy sense of humor and learning to laugh more often. Humor is infectious and the sound of roaring laughter is often contagious. Shared laughter draws people closer together and increases their collective and individual sense of well-being. Humor eases internal and interpersonal tension, lightens your burdens, fosters hope, and builds bonds between people, all the while keeping us grounded. It is, therefore, critically important to schedule fun recreational times into our lives where we can let our hair down and enjoy some laughter with our friends, the belly laugh kind, if you know what I mean. It's also a way you can lift up those in your sphere of influence who are feeling down and out. It's a unique gift you can give to them.

Humor and laughter also hold the power to bolster your immune system, boost your energy, reduce pain, and buffer you from the negative effects of stress. Paul E. McGhee, PhD, says, "Your sense of humor is one of the most powerful tools you have to make certain that your daily mood and emotional state support good health." A good laugh works wonders toward bringing your mind and body back into balance. Laughter can relax the whole body. It boosts the immune system by decreasing stress hormones and increasing immune cells and infection-fighting antibodies, strengthening one's resistance to disease. Furthermore, laughter triggers the release of endorphins, the body's natural "feel-good chemical" which can alleviate pain. It even protects the heart by improving the function of blood vessels and increasing blood flow.

§

Besides the many physical health benefits, laughter also has a number of mental health benefits. It adds joy and zest to life, lessens anxiety and fear, relieves emotional stress, improves mood, and increases resilience. Humor enables you to remain positive and maintain an optimistic outlook when confronted with tough situations, disappointment, and loss. It fuels your courage and sense of hope.

The social benefits of laughter include strengthening relationships through humor and playful communication, attracting others to us to forge positive bonds, enhancing teamwork, soothing conflict, and promoting group closeness. These qualities supply a strong buffer against stress, disagreements, and disappointment.

§

Ella Wheeler Wilcox, in her *Poems of Passion* published in 1883, wrote,

> Laugh, and the world laughs with you;
> Weep, and you weep alone;
> For the sad old earth must borrow its mirth,
> But has trouble enough of its own.

We need to actively seek opportunities to laugh. Some avenues to do this include watching funny (and clean) movies or TV shows, reading the funny pages, spending time with good-humored and fun-loving people, sharing good jokes or humorous stories, hosting game nights with friends, letting your hair down and acting silly, and making time for various fun activities with others.

Meetup groups can provide a wonderful avenue for easing loneliness. It really doesn't matter what the shared activity is as much as simply spending time together. These groups may revolve around interests such as hiking, knitting, painting, cards or dominoes, writing, golfing, gardening, you name it! You may want to consider starting one in your community or in your congregation. People often are lonely and crave non-threatening human interaction and fun.

§

In my way of thinking, life without laughter is a rather miserable way to exist. Laughter has the extraordinary power to open up our minds and hearts to pure exuberance and creative expression as well as to many deeper emotions that may have been previously inaccessible to us. So, stop taking yourself so seriously. Learn to joke and laugh more. Purchase tickets to see a Christian comedian perform like Chonda Pierce, Mark Lowry, or Tim Hawkins. It will be time and money well spent.

As a preacher, I've often embraced Aristotle's oratory principle of "pathos," derived from his classic celebrated work, *Rhetoric* (1515 BCE), which says that if a speaker can get an audience to laugh with him or her, and thereby build a sense of emotional connection and trust with the listeners, he or she will also hold the power in the palm of his/her hands to get the audience to cry with him or her. Laughter removes most emotional barriers and many psychological walls. It serves a valuable function in its inherent capacity to take away unhealthy inhibitions and open up the psyche to new and challenging information. Because laughter generally makes people feel safer and freer to open up their hearts, it allows for increased vulnerability and a childlike, authentic, joy-filled expression.

Isn't it time to tickle your funny bone?

§

Blue Task
#13

- Go on YouTube and search for videos created by hilarious, Christian comedians.
- Find a funny story or a book of jokes to read.
- Find a great joke to tell a friend. Give it a few trial runs in front of the mirror if need be to practice your delivery, especially the punch line.
- Next, seek an opportune moment to give the joke a dry run with a family member. Afterward, you can give the joke a whirl with a friend or even a group of friends.
- You may want to invite a friend or family member to watch a funny movie or a live performance by a clean comedian. If you're feeling extra ambitious, you could organize a fun church group outing to watch a comedic performance.

Chapter Fourteen

☀☁

Stepping Out by Faith

IT'S the Sunday before Thanksgiving week. Henry, a caring minister, has just closed out the morning service and is now standing at the church door greeting and shaking worshippers' hands as they leave. Next in line is a forty-four-year-old divorced mother of two teenagers. She is attempting to smile but her sad eyes tell a different story.

"Hi, Jeanette, how have you been getting along?"

She takes hold of Henry's outstretched hand. "Hello, Pastor. I'm surviving, I suppose."

"Just surviving? What's going on?"

She frowns and tears instantly well up. "It's just the holidays . . . they can be a bit depressing. Too many memories."

Squinting and furrowing his brow, Henry knowingly nods his head. "I understand. It's not been easy for you. Need a hug?"

"Please. That would be nice."

He reaches his arms around her and gently engulfs her in a warm embrace. Upon releasing each other, Jeanette exhales with a sigh. She then produces a well-worn tissue from her pocket to dab away the tears. "Thanks, I really needed that today."

"You're most welcome. I care about you. Please let me know if you'd like to talk sometime this week."

"I'll likely take you up on that offer. It's been a rough year."

"Stop by the office and we'll visit over a fresh cup of coffee."

Her face brightens. "Sounds good." Heartened for the moment, they say their goodbyes as Jeanette heads out the door.

§

While the holidays ought to be a time of good cheer, for many persons they are instead filled with sadness and depression. Holiday celebrations are not only stressful for many; they can also serve as a painful reminder of personal heartaches and losses. Feelings of despair can easily settle in. It's therefore critically important for ministers and members of congregations to be mindful of those in their church families and communities who have recently lost loved ones, struggled with debilitating illnesses, dealt with job loss and financial strain, had their hearts broken due to intimate relationships dissolving, been forced to make difficult decisions such as placing their aging parents in nursing homes, or dealt with painful disappointments over the recent weeks or months.

Therefore, this time of the year presents a unique opportunity for Christians to compassionately serve, comfort, and encourage those around us who need some extra support and encouragement. Be on the lookout for opportunities to reach out to others with your kind smile, listening ear, warm handshake or hug, a thoughtful card or gift, or even an invitation to attend a holiday meal with you and your family. Show the compassion and kindness of Christ and the love and grace of God. Elvis once sang, "I'll have a blue Christmas without you." Let's take positive measures to personally intervene in a person's blueness and help to transform their holiday season into something positive, hope-filled, and memorable.

§

There are several practical things you can do to make a positive difference in others' lives, and in turn in your own life. A simple idea is to begin by asking God to show you who he'd like you to become more aware of within your sphere of influence, so that you may begin praying for them by name. This is a great place to start. It will definitely put your heart in the right place. Then, just see where your heart leads you!

This chapter will offer practical things you can do to make a positive difference in others' lives. Some baby steps offered for your consideration could include any of the following twenty ideas:

1. Write a card to a shut-in, new mother, someone recovering from surgery, or an individual who has lost a loved one or a beloved pet.
2. Make encouraging phone calls to those you are aware of who are struggling in their lives.
3. Develop a prayer list which includes the names of specific individuals whom you want to lift up to God on a regular basis.
4. Volunteer to provide transportation to take a friend or new church member to a book club meeting.
5. Do something thoughtful for your minister's family.
6. Invite a young college student or single adult out for a free meal at a restaurant after church.
7. Make a beautiful flower arrangement for the church.
8. Take your nephew or niece fishing for the day, bowling for the evening, roller skating, or to the movies.
9. Volunteer to take dogs at your local animal shelter for walks.
10. Take donuts to work for your coworkers just because.
11. Purchase a small gift and "thank you" card for the janitor in your workplace to express your gratitude to them for all their hard work.
12. Plant some pretty flowers for an elderly, immobile person and keep them watered.
13. Prepare your spouse's or children's favorite meal.
14. Invite a few shy and less socially active individuals over

to your place for a game night along with cheese dip or chocolate fondue and snacks.

15. Volunteer your services for an evening at a children's home, women's shelter, or soup kitchen.
16. Volunteer to read children's stories to kids at the public library.
17. Visit at a children's hospital and take a craft to make with the young patients.
18. Put together a care package to send to military personnel or missionaries who are stationed/ministering abroad.
19. Pick up trash along a road near where you live.
20. Rake leaves and/or clean debris out of the gutters for an elderly neighbor that needs some assistance.

§

The above ideas are intended to get your creative juices flowing with regard to practical and tangible ways you can get personally involved in good works that make a positive difference in the lives of others, but there are unlimited opportunities to selflessly serve and demonstrate the love and compassion of Christ. The sky's the limit. Brainstorm either by yourself or with a friend and think creatively to come up with your own imaginative ideas.

§

Blue Task
#14

- Select any one of the twenty ideas above or come up with your own fresh ideas, and make plans to implement them, then follow through.

- Be sure to share your ideas with the rest of us on RyanNoelFraser.com under the tab for "Blue Task: Baby Steps Ideas."

Chapter Fifteen

Owning Your Limitations

"I'M just not a big fan of relying on medication," she said. "I've taken some prescription medication in the past for my struggles, but it made me feel weak."

"Do you mean weak physically, emotionally, or something else?" I asked.

"Weak, spiritually," she replied. "It made me feel like a failure in my faith . . . like my faith should be stronger than that. As a Bible class teacher, I really felt like a hypocrite."

"Oh, really. How so?"

"I just felt that if I trusted in the Lord more, I wouldn't have to rely on putting some foreign substance into my body to cope with my problems," she said.

"Okay, I think I understand where you're coming from. But, have you not also considered that God is the One who supplies us with all the raw materials from which medicines are made? Therefore, could we not argue that medicines are also a gift from him provided for our benefit?"

She sniffled as she nodded silently.

§

When I was still an MDiv student at Abilene Christian University, one of my all-time favorite ministry professors was the late Dr. Charles Siburt. I appreciated both him as a person and his class, for a number of reasons. He was authentic and his courses were highly practical. He had a great mantra, which he would quote to his students from time to time. With his low, booming voice he'd exclaim, "Reality is your friend!" I believe what he meant by that statement is that it does nobody any good to live in a fantasy world of denial and not accept the realities of life. Without accepting reality, we're unable to respond in an appropriate and healthy fashion. Unrealistic thinking, myopic vision, and naïveté are rather unhelpful approaches to life and ministry. Similarly, it is tempting for an individual suffering with depression to live in a state of denial about some of the unpleasant realities of their struggle. We can fool others and ourselves into thinking we can operate like everyone else, yet realistically there are real limitations to our physical and emotional energy resources that require proper attention. It is, therefore, vitally important for us to establish and maintain healthy personal boundaries and take appropriate precautions and measures.

It is unwise to subject oneself to stressful situations that may trigger depressive symptoms. Knowing our limitations and when to say "no" is a positive indicator of heightened self-awareness and personal wisdom. Your physical and emotional life are extremely precious to God. If listening to others' sad situations brings you down, it is okay to recommend they speak to someone more qualified than yourself.

§

Where Do Meds Fit In?

Many believers have mixed feelings about taking psychotropic medication to help them alleviate issues like depression and anxiety. However, it is important to take a balanced approach and consider both the pros and cons of using antidepressant and antianxiety medication.

I view prescription drugs as one strategy of treatment for depressive disorder, but there are many additional helpful things a person can do to alleviate some of their own difficulties with mood disorders. I believe that doing so is the most viable and responsible approach. However, that being said, many individuals ultimately do still need some medical assistance to reach a satisfactory level of mental health functioning. In my opinion, God gave us the blessing of capable physicians and nurse practitioners who are there to help us when we need it. God also provided us with the gift of raw natural materials and elements from which the medical scientific community creates medication.

Nonetheless, it can be challenging and a bit frustrating finding the right medication that works best for you. The most common category of antidepressants are called selective serotonin reuptake inhibitors (SSRIs). As a whole, they're considered relatively safe and have fewer side effects than other kinds of antidepressant medication.

§

Types of SSRIs

The Food and Drug Administration (FDA) holds the authority to decided which medications are safe and effective. The FDA has approved the following SSRIs to treat depression, anxiety, and other mood disorders:

- Citalopram (Celexa)
- Escitalopram (Lexapro)
- Fluoxetine (Prozac)
- Fluvoxamine (Luvox, Luvox CR)
- Paroxetine (Paxil, Paxil CR)
- Sertraline (Zoloft)

§

Possible Side Effects

While the majority of people who use SSRI antidepressants don't suffer any significant side effects, it must still be understood that any kind of medical treatment carries at least some level of risk, even if it's relatively small. With that in mind, potential side effects of SSRI antidepressants include the following:

- Agitation or nervousness
- Blurred vision
- Dizziness
- Drowsiness
- Dry mouth
- Gastrointestinal problems including upset stomach or diarrhea
- Headaches
- Insomnia
- Joint or muscle pain
- Nausea
- Problems with erection or ejaculation
- Rash
- Reduced libido (or sexual desire)
- Suicidal thoughts

SSRIs can sometimes have negative interactions with other medicines as well as herbs and supplements, so it is important to notify your doctor of any you're taking, and then proceed with caution. Some individuals, especially children and young adults, may be more prone to experience suicidal thoughts when taking SSRIs. If you entertain serious thoughts of hurting yourself while taking an SSRI, please seek professional help immediately.

While some individuals experience bothersome side effects, others don't have any, and in many cases, side effects go away after a few weeks of treatment. It's important to remain in communication with your doctor to find a medication that works best for you, to slowly build up to the dosage prescribed under your doctor's close supervision, and to decrease slowly if you and your doctor determine that it's necessary to cease the prescription for whatever reason. Though everyone responds a bit differently with regard to enjoying mental improvements due to taking SSRIs, most people start seeing noticeable changes after approximately four to six weeks of treatment, but it may take several months before reaping the full benefit. That being said, if you're not experiencing any significant improvements after about six to eight weeks, make another appointment with your physician to discuss alternate treatment options.

§

Considerations in Stopping Treatment

Although SSRIs aren't habit-forming drugs, it can still be dangerous to suddenly stop taking them or to miss several doses in a row. Doing either of these things may result in a serious condition called "discontinuation syndrome" (also called "antidepressant withdrawal syndrome") that produces withdrawal-like symptoms. Individuals that have discontinuation syndrome may experience flu-like symptoms (such as nausea, vomiting, diarrhea, headaches, and sweating), sleeping difficulties, fatigue or lethargy, dizziness and poor balance, sensory changes, and general uneasiness or anxiety. In rare cases, psychosis may occur. You should not stop taking an SSRI because you are feeling better. Remember, the SSRI is helping you feel better. Major Depressive Disorder is not the flu. It does not have a cure. You do not just get over it. You need to be under the care of a doctor to change or stop your medication.

A number of years ago in a counseling session, a religious leader confessed to me that he was considering resigning his position as a leader in the church because of his ongoing struggle with depression. Upon further inquiry, I learned that he had ceased taking his antidepressants when he began feeling better because he believed that being reliant on psychotropic medication made him spiritually weak. I told him that there would be no need for resignation at this time. Instead, I insisted he set up an appointment with his medical doctor to get back on a regular regimen of antidepressants. We spoke again a few weeks later and his entire countenance had changed for the better. He no longer wanted to quit being a church leader, but could now see things more clearly and recognized that he could use his emotional sensitivity to help those around him. He continued to serve as a good shepherd. Keep in mind that the process of finding the right medication may often involve a significant amount of trial and error under doctor supervision and may require tenacity and patience on your part before you find the best combination for you, but prescribed medication and professional psychotherapy can play a vital role in one's recovery.

§

Blue Task
#15

- If the symptoms of your blueness fall more into the realm of a clinical depression, (i.e., you live in a constant state of violet blue or dark indigo), set up an appointment to talk with your physician about your symptoms and, with your their help, decide if you require medication.

Chapter Sixteen

Counselee Becoming a Counselor

OFTEN hiding behind a façade of "having it all together" and fake happiness are those who are depressed, fearful, and anxious. Godly counselors are needed now, more than ever, in the church to lend a trustworthy and confidential listening ear, provide a sounding board, and offer sage advice. The work of Christian counselors ought to be a role and responsibility shared with the congregation among its lay leaders and members.

Jesus understood the vulnerability of the human condition and therefore directly addressed the specific issues that people were dealing with in their lives. Our caring service is to primarily be a spiritual work that occurs only by the power of God and through the wisdom and grace of the living and active Word of God. To console someone is to help them make it through an extremely painful experience of sadness or disappointment by offering our sincere sympathy and emotional support. During Jesus's ministry, we observe a number of instances when he directly provided consolation to people who needed it desperately. The care of consolation appears to always be closely linked with the giving or sharing of "good news" (i.e., gospel).

Going into such a level of care is for the person that has over a period of time successfully navigated the smaller steps in reaching out to care for others. Because of your firsthand experience of depression, you are attuned to the emotional needs of others. Who better to become a capable, godly counselor and/or support group facilitator than you?

§

As much as possible, the body of Christ needs to view itself as a community of care in which many capable counselors are willing and available to lend a hand whenever it is necessary. The truth of the matter is that the most commonly occurring counseling happens most often in impromptu situations. It takes place at the beauty salon or barbershop, in the dugout at the ball field or in the stands or by the concession stand. It transpires in the hallway of the school building, in the lunchroom or by the vending machine at the workplace, or even out in the parking lot. And it is done by compassionate laypersons that simply take the time to listen and empathize with those who are struggling in some way.

Psalm 1:1-2 (ESV) states, "Blessed is the man who walks not in the counsel of the wicked, nor stands in the way of sinners, nor sits in the seat of scoffers; but his delight is in the law of the LORD, and on his law he meditates day and night." Plenty of ungodly and unspiritual advice is readily available by nonbelievers in the secular world. Christians are, therefore, desperately needed to step up to the plate. There are people stranded on base who need to be brought home. We need to pray for the spiritual wisdom that God promises to all those who ask in faith (James 1:5), so that we as Christians may adequately respond to the counseling needs of others.

Proverbs 11:14 (ESV) exclaims, "Where there is no guidance, a people falls, but in the abundance of counselors there is safety." A web of wisdom provides a safety net of support. Jesus Christ was and remains the "Wonderful Counselor" (Isaiah 9:6), who perfectly modeled through his earthly ministry how we too can become effective Christian caregivers and counselors. Our

Lord took time to listen and thoughtfully respond to those who needed his help and insight. For example, in Luke 12:13 we read of how a man pled with Jesus: "Teacher, tell my brother to divide the inheritance with me" (ESV). This individual was clearly upset about the family squabble he was having with his sibling. Jesus's prudent response in verse 14 (ESV) was, "Man, who made me a judge or arbitrator over you?" The Lord knew that it was unwise to meddle in somebody else's personal family affairs. He also, however, seized on this opportunity for a teaching moment. Jesus told those present, including the man, "Take care, and be on your guard against all covetousness, for one's life does not consist in the abundance of his possessions" (v. 15, ESV). This statement was followed by a parable regarding a rich man who was greatly blessed and became greedy and self-reliant, wanting to hoard his grain and build bigger barns. The fact that the man was wealthy was not the real issue as much as his worldly attitude regarding his riches. This self-satisfied character in the parable said to his soul, "Soul, you have ample goods laid up for many years; relax, eat, drink, be merry" (Luke 12:19b, ESV). But God had other plans. The man's life was about to end and then his earthly treasures would become somebody else's, because he was not rich towards God (vv. 20-21). Jesus, then, went on to address the issue of anxiety regarding material things and how his disciples ought to trust in God who would provide for their every single material need, including food, drink, and clothing (vv. 22-31).

§

Life is hard. People struggle daily with a variety of depressing difficulties and perplexing problems. Jesus understood the vulnerability of the human condition and, therefore, directly addressed the specific issues that people were dealing with in their lives. Most people in churches who are hurting and reaching out for help recognize that there is a spiritual dimension to their problems. Their faith informs them that God's intervention is needed in finding a true and lasting solution.

There are seven essentials to a successful approach toward Christian counseling. **First, lean on the Lord Jesus Christ.** It is arrogant on our part to think we are able to fix somebody else's problems by relying on our own power. Left to our own devices, we tend to make a big mess of things. During my years of teaching at a Christian-affiliated university in the clinical mental health counseling and pastoral care and counseling programs, I've developed a tradition each and every semester with my new counseling students. I instruct the entire class to stand up with me at the beginning of each semester during our second session of class. I then tell them that what I'm about to share with them is of the utmost importance for their survival as helpers so as to avoid burnout. It is something I never want them to forget.

Here it is: I want them to understand at the intellectual, emotional, and spiritual levels that they can't "fix" anybody. Only God possesses the power to bind up the brokenhearted and mend people's broken hearts and beleaguered souls. The best we can hope for is to humbly participate in the work that God is already doing in people's lives to the best of our abilities.

I then have my wide-eyed students repeat the following words after me several times, each time with increasing volume and gusto, until I'm sufficiently convinced that the sentiment has adequately soaked deeply into their psyches: "There is only one Savior, and I am not He!" Go ahead and say it to yourself, preferably out loud, right now. Now say it again a bit louder. And once more with all your might. Are you fully convinced yet?

Counselors-in-training must very early on in their education come to grips with the very real limitations of their own finitude as flawed, mortal human beings. It is crucial that we recognize our complete reliance upon God's help to be able to effectively help others. Just as Jesus frequently went off alone to commune with his Father in prayer in order to receive strength, wisdom, and guidance, so must we (See Matt. 14:23; 26:36-44; Mark 6:46; 14:32-39; Luke 5:16; 6:12; 9:18, 28-29; 11:1; 22:39-45). While we can't bring inner healing to anybody, God certainly has the power to do so and is able to work through us if we will allow him to guide us. Prior to, during, and after counseling sessions, tap into God's unlimited power and pray for wisdom. It's needed to understand how best to proceed, to know what to say, and to discern what to avoid. Sometimes we can say too much!

Second, honor and uphold appropriate legal and ethical boundaries or legal limits related to confidentiality. Certainly, we must always be careful to keep personal information shared by someone with us in strict confidence whenever possible. However, if an individual comes to you and says, "I need to tell you something, but you must promise me ahead of time that you will keep it a secret," please proceed with caution. My standard response is: "While I understand the importance of keeping things private, I can only ensure confidentiality within the limitations placed upon me by the law. For example, if somebody is intending to hurt him- or herself or is actively planning to harm someone else, or if child abuse is brought up, I am required to report it. But, outside those kinds of dangerous situations, I will do my best to keep what you tell me completely confidential."

Third, listen nonjudgmentally and reflectively. When someone is sharing their deepest concerns with us, they need our supportive and undivided attention to what they are saying, so that they will know we are there for them. They need to be assured that no matter what they share with us, we will continue to respect them as a person and care about them. It makes it more difficult for individuals to reveal what is weighing heavily on their hearts if they feel like they are going to be negatively perceived or thought less of by us in some way. While we, like Jesus, must hate the sin, we must also never stop loving the sinner.

When we are listening, it is important to pay close attention to both their verbal statements and nonverbal cues. We must ask thoughtful and respectful questions to gain understanding and clarification and regularly reflect back to the counselee (or care-seeker) what it is we are hearing and understanding them to say. These reflections ought to come not only in the form of our paraphrasing the basic content of their statements, but also in unearthing the underlying feelings (or emotions) associated with their words, and, lastly, the deeper meanings of their statements. In other words, what is it that really is at stake for them? We can thereby help the care-seeker grow in self-awareness as we serve as a sounding board and a mirror to them, helping them to see themselves more clearly.

Fourth, uncover personal strengths they already possess, and look for hidden, positive exceptions that are embedded within the problem-saturated stories they are sharing with us. In other words, when listening to another's problems, it is helpful for us to highlight the special abilities, talents, and competencies as well as the valuable personal characteristics you observe in them. These strengths may be helpful resources they can put to work in resolving their problems. By "exceptions," I am referring to finding out more about specific times in which the person has, in the past (preferably in more recent days), managed to effectively cope with their difficulties to some level of satisfaction. It is important to have them describe the specifics of how they managed to experience small (or even significant) victories over their problems and how they could perhaps duplicate some of those same steps and strategies in the near future.

With Christians, I will often remind them of what the apostle Paul states in 1 Corinthians 10:13, "No temptation has overtaken you that is not common to man. God is faithful, and he will not let you be tempted beyond your ability, but with the temptation he will also provide the way of escape, that you may be able to endure it." The point here is to recognize that God is already at work in their lives to aid them in finding a viable solution to their difficulties. You may ask the care-seeker what small glimpses or signs of God's abiding presence and help they have already been noticing with regard to overcoming their problem. What window of escape is God already opening up to them?

Fifth, recognize your own counseling deficiencies. Resist the temptation to offer quick and easy solutions or to make hasty recommendations. Doing so will likely foster an overly dependent relationship with you rather than empowering the counselee to find their own solutions within their personal frame of reference and social and family context. It is likely that others have already offered them plenty of well-meaning advice that they have either tried or promptly ignored. Therefore, avoid giving any advice prematurely.

Moreover, whenever we give advice we run the real risk of the person actually following our recommendations and it ending disastrously. In this scenario, we could be held responsible for their situation deteriorating as opposed to improving. When advice is given it ought to be offered sparingly and tentatively rather than as if we know all the answers. We want to avoid at all costs assuming the role of an "expert" instead of a fellow struggler and trustworthy confidant.

Furthermore, if necessary we should be prepared to refer those we are trying to help to other more experienced layperson helpers or Christian mental health professionals. We must avoid biting off more than we can chew! Perhaps we will recognize after hearing the person initially share their story that we are ill-equipped to help them due to our own lack of specialized knowledge or experience. Not even the most well-trained counselor or minister has all the answers to every single one of life's perplexing problems. Acknowledging our own mortality, recognizing our limitations, and knowing when we are getting in over our heads is important. Know when to refer!

Sixth, draw out spiritual and theological themes that are woven within the tapestry of the counselee's story. When someone is sharing their story with you, they may overlook significant spiritual or religious pieces to the puzzle that might be essential in finding adequate answers and viable solutions. Think theologically and religiously about the matter they are presenting as well as about the psychological and emotional components that may be involved. Do your best to link the individual's lived experiences and story to the grand themes and hope-filled narratives of God's Word. Doing so might help the person gain spiritual insight into his or her own trials and tribulations. As they contemplate the real human difficulties faced by certain faithful biblical characters and think about how these figures managed to deal with their problems, it may build courage, instill hope, and nurture love.

Seventh, learn from the counselee. We must be humble and open to them teaching us something of value that could make a positive difference in our own life. Strive to build a collaborative relationship where there is mutual respect and their human dignity is preserved. When an individual is in a "one down" position (i.e., they are having to ask for your help) it could make them feel embarrassed and weak and may erode their self-esteem. Therefore, it is important for them to recognize that we view them as someone who can contribute something worthwhile to others and to us through their knowledge, experience, and talents. We must take the humble stance of a student who may stand to learn some helpful lessons and gain valuable insights from them just as they can from us. This way, there will be a reciprocal blessing by which both parties may benefit and grow. Proverbs 27:17 (NIV) says, "As iron sharpens iron, so one man sharpens another."

§

Take note of these seven key concepts for lay Christian counselors, all beginning with the letter "C."

1. Compassionate

Empathy and sympathy both play an important role in Christian counseling. Empathy has to do with understanding the counselee's perspective and struggle. It also includes a non-judgmental attitude. Sympathy has to do with feeling genuine concern for their well-being, just as Jesus demonstrated in Matthew 9:36 (ESV): "When he saw the crowds, he had compassion for them, because they were harassed and helpless, like sheep without a shepherd." Thus, Jesus was touched by the common people's imperiled situation and difficult plight.

2. Connection (contact)

Often, for care-seekers, just feeling like a caring brother or sister in Christ is actually listening and concerned is of immense value and comfort. Basic nonverbals that demonstrate you are paying attention to the person are important (eye contact, head nods, "uh-huhs," minimal encouragers like "okay," "Mmm," "wow"). Good listening skills are critically important, as well as invitational skills or door openers such as "How can I help you?" "Tell me more about that." "What else?" Basic attending skills like paraphrasing, reflecting feelings, reflecting meaning, using clarifying questions, or summarizing what the individual is trying to communicate are also extremely valuable to them.

3. Christ-centered

Second Corinthians 1:3-4 (ESV) says, "Blessed be the God and Father of our Lord Jesus Christ, the Father of mercies and God of all comfort, who comforts us in all our affliction, so that we may be able to comfort those who are in any affliction, with the comfort with which we ourselves are comforted by God." Emphasize Christ's interest in the sufferer and deep love for them. Introduce relevant teachings by Jesus and explore his example for us as it relates to various difficult situations. Introduce biblical themes and faith-based spiritual tools such as worship, prayer, fasting, and meditation on Scripture.

4. Confidential

It is important that the person feels he or she can trust you with their private, personal information and secrets. It gives them a sense of safety in sharing. But there are limits to confidentiality and exceptions to it including the following: child abuse, elderly abuse, suicidal ideation, intent to injure someone else, or federal crime.

5. Competency-based

Focus on the counselee's strengths, abilities, knowledge, and lived experience. Be solution-oriented and capitalize on the counselee's ability to think for themselves, be creative, and make wise decisions. Help them realize that they are competent and possess the requisite skills (or can develop them) to achieve satisfactory resolution to their presenting problems.

6. Collaborative

Demonstrate a respectful attitude that affords the counselee appropriate human dignity. Develop a caring relationship that emphasizes the value of Christian fellowship and shared responsibility. Work together to develop appropriately concrete and realistic goals for counseling, along with a strategy to reach these goals. Develop a sense of teamwork.

7. Cognitive-behavioral

This model of counseling revolves around Thinking, Feeling, and Doing. Explore how the counselee's cognition (Thinking)—especially irrational or illogical thoughts—are impacting their emotions (Feelings), and in turn affecting their behavior (Doing). Challenge fallacious and irrational thoughts about others, self, and God. Help the individual find alternative, healthier interpretations of what is happening and why it's happening.

§

Using God's Word in Counseling

Biblically sound counseling should include taking God's Word seriously and using it appropriately to help provide direction to the counselee regarding his or her difficulties. In secular circles, people often take issue with the concept of integrating theology and psychology. I personally take issue with it when it is not done properly. We need to learn how theology and psychology best work together. After all, if all wisdom ultimately belongs to God, so do the professional disciplines of psychology and counseling. It is important to be well prepared to employ Scripture in counseling in an appropriate and beneficial way.

First things first. It is essential from the start that we determine if the care-seeker is comfortable with our use of the Bible in counseling. If they are, we must then use Scripture *scripturally*. At first glance, this statement almost sounds redundant,but it isn't when correctly understood. What I am saying is that we must be sure that we are employing the Bible in the right manner and within its proper context. We must avoid proof-texting and distorting the Bible to say something we want it to say, but that it really doesn't say at all. Thus, it is important to read and interpret the Bible using adequate hermeneutical (i.e., interpretation) principles such as the following:

1. Who is the author?
2. What type of writing is this: historical, poetic/wisdom literature, law, prophecy, gospel, letter/epistle, etc.?
3. To whom is the author writing and for what original intent or purpose?
4. What is the larger context of the specific text we are seeking to interpret?

5. How is the text best understood in its historical context and larger biblical and sociocultural setting?

6. What does the Bible say elsewhere that may help interpret or shed light on the present text?

7. What spiritual principles and behaviors ought to be taken from it and applied to our contemporary setting?

§

We must also be careful to use Scripture *psychologically*. By this statement I mean that we ought to employ it in such a way that it attends to the individual's psychological and emotional needs, not just their intellectual understanding. Hebrews 4:12 (ESV) states, "For the word of God is living and active, sharper than any two-edged sword, piercing to the division of soul and of spirit, of joints and of marrow, and discerning the thoughts and intentions of the heart." Thus, the Bible possesses the inherent power to cut us to the quick. It is able to both build up and tear down a person's psyche depending on the situation and need.

Therefore, the Bible ought to be used and applied in a positive and appropriate psychological way. Simply quoting or reading a scripture doesn't necessarily make for effective biblical counseling. Remember that when Satan quoted Scripture to Jesus during the temptations described in Matthew 4:1-11, he distorted and twisted it for his own evil purposes. Jeffrey Watson states, "When the devil quoted words from the Bible to Jesus, he was not offering biblical counsel. When he baited the Lord to turn bricks to bread, to free-fall from the high Jerusalem wall, and to kiss the ring of evil, he was not engaged in the art of biblical counseling though Psalm 91 was on his lips."[10]

§

---

10 Watson, Jeffrey. *Biblical Counseling for Today: A Handbook for Those Who Counsel from Scripture*. Nashville: Word, 2000.

So, how is one to go about appropriately using Scripture in a counseling situation? It will help to ask the following questions of oneself:

1. Who is the person sitting in front of me and what is important to them?
2. What has their experience with the Bible been thus far in their lives?
3. Do they view the Bible as a source of comfort or does it conjure up painful memories for them?
4. What is the counselee's specific context in which they live, namely their cultural and family traditions, present lifestyle and problems, as well as their past history?
5. What biblical passages might speak more effectively to this particular person given their unique cultural environment and background?
6. What word from God does this person most need to hear presently in their life?
7. Does the message connect with them where they are or does it only tell them where we think they ought to be?
8. Why do I want to share this particular biblical passage with them (i.e., What is my agenda or hidden motivation)?
9. What do I hope to accomplish by sharing this scripture (to provoke, challenge, teach, or comfort)?
10. What would be the best manner in which to deliver or communicate this message to them?
11. What barriers could hinder the counselee from grasping the intended meaning of the inspired biblical passage?
12. How might they possibly misconstrue my intentions in sharing this scripture?[11]

---

11 Pate, Stephen. "How to Use Scripture in Counseling." Unpublished honors paper in the Family and Individual Counseling course. Henderson, TN: Freed-Hardeman University, 2008.

§

Our task in Christian counseling is to help care-seekers reconstruct the perceptions they hold of their problems by creating new possibilities for abundant life beyond the problems that bind and constrict. Charles Kollar states, "Helping counselees to get unstuck and back on track is a way in which God's Spirit begins to heal."[12] Our task is not to see this work of God all the way through to completion but only to participate with God in removing the veils from people's eyes so they too can discern God's presence.

Howard Stone[13] challenges us to remember that when it comes to counseling, our first and foremost task is a spiritual one, not a psychological one. We are to always look through a theological lens to inform the healing, guiding, sustaining, and reconciling we endeavor to bring about. As caregivers, our primary frame of reference must be the Word of God that resides in the community of faith. This Word is not only that which is visibly fleshed out in our doing but also that which is grappled with in our listening and voiced in our speaking. James (1:22, NIV) writes: "Do not merely listen to the word, and so deceive yourselves. Do what it says." Christian counseling is a call both to actively listen to the Word and a call to positive action—to live out the kingdom life portrayed within the Bible by our deeds.

Our caring service is to primarily be a spiritual work that occurs only by the power of God and through the wisdom and grace of the living and active Word of God. To faithfully integrate this Word into our Christian caring, we must be drinking deeply of it ourselves, so that we are constantly being transformed into

12 Kollar, Charles Allen. *Solution-Focused Pastoral Counseling: An Effective Short-Term Approach for Getting People Back on Track.* Grand Rapids: Zondervan, 1997.

13 Stone, Howard W. *Theological Context for Pastoral Counseling: Word in Deed.* Binghamton, NY: Haworth, 1996.

the image of Christ. Only then will our integration of spiritual disciplines into the care we offer be truly grace-filled and effective. And only then will these divine resources be perceived as helpful and authentic to the counselees.

Scripture has the powerful potential to inform and transform the thinking, understanding, and attitudes of those individuals who are facing seemingly insurmountable obstacles in their lives. It can either build up or tear down depending on the needs of the present circumstances. When we promote a greater interest in the Bible within those whom we are trying to help, more individuals will be referred to the Wonderful Counselor who is able to teach, heal, and comfort the sufferer as no one else can. Now, my Missy is a caring school counselor. She has learned to live with her depressive disorder. As a counselor, she often reaches the unreachable child because of—not in spite of—her depression, which heightens her sensitivity toward others' emotional needs. I am proud of how she makes such a positive difference in the lives of struggling children and parents.

On a side note: As a result of your own journey toward greater emotional and spiritual healing from depression, you may have developed a significant interest in seeking more formal training in becoming a certified and/or licensed Christian counselor. I want to encourage you to seek additional information about pursuing that career path, through which you will be able to help many other sufferers discover psycho-spiritual comfort and hope.

§

Blue Task
#16

- Not everyone can be, or wants to be, a professional counselor, but you can practice being a nonjudgmental listening ear to a friend, family member, or colleague. Reach out to someone you know who is struggling. Invite them out for coffee. Ask them how they are doing. Take the time to really listen and show compassion.

- If you are interested in becoming a Christian counselor, or at least finding out more about the educational requirements and training options, do some online research concerning various available graduate programs. I may be a little biased, but I would highly recommend the graduate Clinical Mental Health Counseling program at Freed-Hardeman University, as well as the MA in Pastoral Care and Counseling. Go to fhu.edu for more information.

- Seek out articles and/or books on the topic of pastoral counseling and/or Christian counseling to broaden your awareness and deepen your understanding. I highly recommend the following resources:

  - *Brief Pastoral Counseling: Short-term Approaches and Strategies* by Howard W. Stone, Fortress Press, 1993.

  - *Christian Counseling: A Comprehensive Guide*, 3rd ed. by Gary R. Collins, Thomas Nelson Publishers, 2007.

  - *Solution-Focused Pastoral Counseling: An Effective Short-Term Approach for Getting People Back on Track*, deluxe edition by Charles Allen Kollar, Zondervan Publishing House, 2011.

- *Strategic Pastoral Counseling: A Short-Term Structured Model*, 2nd ed. by David G. Benner, Baker Academic, 2003.
- *The Quick-Reference Guide to Biblical Counseling* by Tim Clinton and Ron Hawkins, Baker Books, 2009.

Chapter Seventeen

☁

The Blue Servant

FEELING blue? God still has a plan for you! He has foreordained a special purpose for your life—an important work he's prepared in advance for you to tackle, a meaningful mission for you to accomplish. Ephesians 2:10 (ESV) says, "For we are his workmanship, created in Christ Jesus for good works, which God prepared beforehand, that we should walk in them." Isn't that encouraging to know? God has always intended for *you* to be a difference maker in this world. Please never lose sight of that spiritual reality, because a whole lot is riding on it for you and for others! Everyone in God's family has a purpose, a job to do. We are all needed. You are needed.

At the beginning of this book, I tried to make the point that just because you struggle with depression doesn't make you less-than, spiritually weak, or unworthy in your service to God. God might, in fact, be able to work through your lived experience by redeeming your story in such a way as to bring about much good. However, you've got to decide whether you're going to be a willing participant in his plan for your life or not, because he'll never force you to embrace his divine will for your life.

To be a "blue servant" means to have a *renewed* mind, a *refocused* vision, a *revived* spirit, a *restored* or *resurrected* hope, a *revitalized* joy, and *reprioritized* agenda. In Ezekiel 37:3, God asks the prophet "Son of man, can these bones live?" The powerful vision of Ezekiel continues with a prophecy of resurrection and restoration for the people of Israel. The biblical narrative states the following in verses 1–6 (ESV):

> [1] The hand of the Lord was upon me, and he brought me out in the Spirit of the Lord and set me down in the middle of the valley; it was full of bones. [2] And he led me around among them, and behold, there were very many on the surface of the valley, and behold, they were very dry. [3] And he said to me, "Son of man, can these bones live?" And I answered, "O Lord God, you know." [4] Then he said to me, "Prophesy over these bones, and say to them, O dry bones, hear the word of the Lord. [5] Thus says the Lord God to these bones: Behold, I will cause breath to enter you, and you shall live. [6] And I will lay sinews upon you, and will cause flesh to come upon you, and cover you with skin, and put breath in you, and you shall live, and you shall know that I am the Lord."

The clear and vivid message is that there is hope for God's people, just as there is hope for you. Your depressed and dry bones will live again. Yes, through the resurrection power of God, they will be reanimated for a greater purpose if you are willing. The blue servant is one who is sensitive to the needs of others, keenly aware of one's own very real limitations of time, energy, and expertise, humble in one's own self-appraisal, but one who is nonetheless willing to be available and receptive to God's leading and call. The blue servant recognizes his or her own weaknesses, while grasping onto God's almighty hand. In 2 Corinthians 12:9-10 (ESV), the apostle Paul reflects on God's response to his ardent prayer for deliverance and healing:

> [9] But he said to me, "My grace is sufficient for you, for my power is made perfect in weakness." Therefore I

will boast all the more gladly of my weaknesses, so that the power of Christ may rest upon me. [10]For the sake of Christ, then, I am content with weaknesses, insults, hardships, persecutions, and calamities. For when I am weak, then I am strong.

The blue servant also comprehends and embraces the length, width, height, and depth of God's unwavering love. In Ephesians 3:16-19 (ESV), Paul says:

> [16]that according to the riches of his glory he may grant you to be strengthened with power through his Spirit in your inner being, [17]so that Christ may dwell in your hearts through faith—that you, being rooted and grounded in love, [18]may have strength to comprehend with all the saints what is the breadth and length and height and depth, [19]and to know the love of Christ that surpasses knowledge, that you may be filled with all the fullness of God.

To be blue is to be beloved. To be blue is to be bold and beautiful. To be blue is to remain useful to God. To be blue is to be set apart for a special holy purpose for God's glory. So, fear not! Step out by faith and become a faithful blue servant and make a positive difference in this world!

And with regard to God's plans for you, I absolutely love what Jeremiah 29:11 (NIV) promises: "For I know the plans I have for you," declares the LORD, plans to prosper you and not to harm you, plans to give you hope and a future."

Whatever you decide to do or not do as a result of reading this book, please hold onto hope. Don't give up on God. He certainly hasn't given up on you.

§

Blue Task
#11

- Regardless of whether you're artistic or not, draw a picture depicting you as a "blue servant" making a positive difference in the lives of others. You may add descriptive words to your masterpiece if you feel like it.
- I would love for you to upload a photo of your work of art on your social media sites with the hashtag #blueservant.
- Alternatively, you may take a photograph related to a personal service project you've undertaken to help others and post it on your social media sites with the hashtag #blueservant. It will serve as a huge encouragement to the rest of us!

Epilogue

I'M not sure what you were expecting to find when you picked up this book for the very first time. I hope it has surprised you and come as a breath of fresh air to your soul. My prayer is that it has already served as a source of great spiritual blessing and encouragement to you and that it will continue to do so in your life and in the lives of those around you.

This book is not intended, in any way, to be a replacement for proper medical attention and professional therapeutic services. One of my purposes in writing this work was for it to serve as a practical, Bible-based, spiritually-informed, God-centered supplement to that which the medical and psychotherapeutic community offers by way of specialized care. I urge you to seek appropriate help from your physician or a licensed professional counselor if necessary.

However, that being said, I hope you see the inherent value in this book and that you will be a courageous advocate of its message by sharing its novel and innovative contents with your friends, family, colleagues, and acquaintances who might stand to benefit from it. You could very well serve as a catalyst to get a support group started in your community or church that uses the contents of *Overcoming the Blues* for educational and encouragement purposes. Perhaps you will choose to discuss this possibility with one of the ministry leaders in your congregation in order to explore various options that may best fit your context. Please keep in mind there is also a supplemental teacher's/group leader's discussion guide, student workbook, and chapter-by-chapter video series that accompany this book, as well as several user-friendly resources available on my website, RyanNoelFraser.com. Look under "Blues Supplemental Resources."

Isn't time for you to step out of the dark shadows, which often envelope your heart and psyche, and begin reaching upward to the light of Christ and outward into the lives of others? With God's help, you can be transformed mentally, emotionally, and spiritually by the renewal of your mind (see Romans 12:1-2) and mobilized for valuable and life-changing kingdom service. Don't allow your blueness or depression to hold you back from using your talents and opportunities to do good deeds! I challenge you to keep plugging away and moving forward, step-by-step. *No matter what!*

§

Let's start a #blueservant movement together to change the status quo in the church and society by informing and transforming present understandings among believers regarding the disease of depression. Together, let's seek to promote biblically sound strategies to cope with the blues more effectively and live more victoriously. I challenge you to decide right here and now to become a courageous advocate and proactive voice for those who suffer with depression, and to be a positive change agent in the church. Let's turn the problem of the presence of the blues into a powerful platform for meaningful Christian service to others.

Just because you're feeling blue does not mean God can't use you in remarkable ways for his glory and honor. In fact, the exact opposite is true. He has prepared special works of service for you to do since before the foundation of the world (Eph. 2:10). Marvelous, magnificent, and meaningful works of service in the lives of others can make a positive difference and provide you with a deep sense of satisfaction and fulfillment. Hope is on the horizon, so please don't lose heart or give up.

Appendix

MAJOR depressive disorder can develop at any age; however, the average age at onset is 32.[14] What you might not know is that depression is the leading cause of disability in the US for ages 15-44.[15]

Furthermore, antidepressants have become the second highest volume drug in the US, second only to cholesterol medication. It's definitely mindboggling to grasp that the number of people diagnosed with depression is increasing by 30% every year. And, it is important to recognize that depressive disorders often co-occur with anxiety disorders and substance abuse.[16] On a global scale, reportedly more than 350 million people of all ages worldwide suffer with depression.[17]

---

14 Kessler, R. C., Berglund, P. A., Demler, O., Jin, R., & Walters, E. E. Lifetime prevalence and age-of-onset distributions of DSM-IV disorders in the National Comorbidity Survey Replication (NCS-R). *Archives of General Psychiatry*, 2005, June, *62(6)*: 593-602.

15 The World Health Organization. *The global burden of disease: 2004 update*, Table A2: Burden of disease in DALYs by cause, sex and income group in WHO regions, estimates for 2004. Geneva, Switzerland: WHO, 2008.

16 See footnote #4. Kessler, R. C., Berglund, P. A., Demler, O., Jin, R., & Walters, E. E. Lifetime prevalence and age-of-onset distributions of DSM-IV disorders in the National Comorbidity Survey Replication (NCS-R). *Archives of General Psychiatry*, 2005, June, *62(6)*: 593-602.

17 World Health Organization (WHO), Fact sheet N°369, October 2012. ©WHO 2014. http://www.who.int/mediacentre/factsheets/fs369/en/

Countless individuals battle this formidable foe on a daily basis often in silence, secrecy, and shame. The sad reality is that depression is more often than not at the root of many, if not most, suicide attempts and deaths by suicide. Regrettably, the majority of us have been touched either directly or indirectly by the suicide of a loved one.

We can confidently say that people *everywhere* are hurting and in desperate need of real help, but not just any help—help that addresses mind, body, and soul—help that provides hope and comfort for the faithful Christian. So, here's a thought to ponder: What if the depressed person might offer help to another person and, in that process, help him or herself at the same time? Wouldn't that constitute a double blessing?

The avenue of compassionate caring and serving is a relatively untapped strategy or antidote for depressed persons to facilitate their own healing and growth. Rather than advancing secular approaches to caregiving, though they definitely are needed and have their rightful place, this book seeks to *motivate*, *mentor*, and *mobilize* sufferers of depression in the church to become effectual, Christ-centered, joy-filled compassion givers. To find a path to come out of themselves and discover newfound hope and purpose.

Acknowledgments

I'M indebted to a number of special people for the successful achievement of writing this book. First of all, I want to thank my beautiful wife, Missy. You have taught me far more than anyone else has about the real struggle of depression and how to press on through the pain to find meaningful purpose. My young adult children, Olivia and Austin, and my son-in-law Dalen, have been a great source of encouragement. Also, my extended family on the Fraser and Housel sides have consistently demonstrated support along the way.

I'm exceedingly thankful for the congregations in which I grew up in South Africa and the wonderful people who helped to shape my faith at the Bellville and Milnerton churches of Christ. Then, there are all those kind-hearted and patient individuals at the congregations I've been blessed to serve as a minister, deacon, and elder over the past thirty-one years, including Milledgeville Church of Christ (Milledgeville, Tennessee), Adams Boulevard Church of Christ (Bartlesville, Oklahoma), Faith Village Church of Christ (Wichita Falls, Texas), Henrietta Church of Christ (Henrietta, Texas), North Jackson Church of Christ (Jackson, Tennessee), and more recently the close-knit group of believers at Bethel Springs Church of Christ (Bethel Springs, Tennessee).

I deeply appreciate Dr. Howard W. Stone and the tremendous opportunity he afforded me to gain valuable experience in the classroom as his teacher assistant while completing my doctoral studies in Pastoral Theology and Pastoral Counseling at Brite Divinity School (Texas Christian University) in Fort Worth. I've always valued our warm camaraderie and your professional mentorship.

It has been a blessing over the past thirteen years (since 2006) to serve on the Clinical Mental Health Counseling faculty at Freed-Hardeman University. My esteemed colleagues in the Department of Behavioral Sciences are phenomenal human beings. I appreciate each of you so very much. Now, as I transition over to the College of Biblical Studies at FHU, I'm excited about the possibilities and distinct honor and privilege of working side by side with such a talented team of colleagues.

Diana Flegal, my phenomenal literary agent at Hartline Literary, has stuck by my side through many ups and downs over the past five years, while striving to get this work written and published. Thanks for keeping the faith and for never giving up on me or our shared vision for this ambitious project. The devil is definitely not happy with us! You have been a true godsend. I'm also very grateful to Nicole Mele, my gifted editor at Skyhorse Publishing, for taking a big chance on me as a relatively unknown author. You and your team are simply amazing!

I deeply appreciate all the board members of His Heart, My Hands Inc. (a newly-formed non-profit 501c3 charitable organization) for your personal commitment to this project and your willingness to step up and live out the central theme of this book by selflessly and joyfully serving others. We're all on this journey together!

Last, but most importantly, I thank my gracious and merciful God in heaven for providing me with the incredible opportunity to share the message of this book with the world. Your divine fingerprints have been so evident all throughout my life to bring me to this moment by preparing me and clearing the path for this great adventure. You are forever faithful and true. "Now to him who is able to do immeasurably more than all we ask or imagine, according to his power that is at work within us, to him be glory in the church and in Christ Jesus throughout all generations, for ever and ever! Amen" (Ephesians 3:20-21, NIV).

Index